WAR ON WORDS

THE WAR ON WORDS

10 Arguments Against FREE SPEECH—And Why They Fail

Greg Lukianoff &
Nadine Strossen
Foreword by Jacob Mchangama

Heresy Press books may be purchased in bulk at special discounts for sales promotion, corporate gifts, fund-raising, or educational purposes. Special editions can also be created to specifications. For details, contact the Special Sales Department, Skyhorse Publishing, 307 West 36th Street, 11th Floor, New York, NY 10018 or info@skyhorsepublishing.com.

Skyhorse Publishing® is a registered trademark of Skyhorse Publishing, Inc.®, a Delaware corporation.

Visit our website at skyhorsepublishing.com.

HERESY PRESS
P.O. Box 425201
Cambridge, MA 02142
heresy-press.com

Heresy Press is an imprint of Skyhorse Publishing.

10 9 8 7 6 5 4 3 2 1

Library of Congress Cataloging-in-Publication Data is available on file.

Jacket design by David Ter-Avanesyan

ISBN: 978–1-949846–82-9
Ebook ISBN: 978–1-949846–83-6

Printed in the United States of America

Contents

Foreword

by Jacob Mchangama

Nadine Strossen and Greg Lukianoff have undertaken a monumental and crucial task by systematically refuting the "10 arguments against" free speech most frequently advanced by those who think this freedom has gone too far and should be restricted.

It's about time too! Because the history of free speech demonstrates that the "10 arguments against" that Strossen and Lukianoff identify are not modern inventions: one or more of them have—in various guises—been used to justify censorship and repression throughout history and around the world by oligarchies, theocracies, dictatorships and, yes, democratic governments on the left, right, and center.

Modern, conscientious liberals may think they are the first to consider "words as violence" (Argument #1). Yet, as I've written in *Free Speech: A History from Socrates to Social Media*, English apologists for Charles I blamed the "Paper Bullets of the Press" for the English Civil War that led to Charles's beheading.[1] After prepublication censorship was repealed in 1695, British Tories, alarmed by the "licentiousness" of the press, warned that seditious libelers were the "very Assassins of all Government," and that "a Civil War began with Ink may end in Blood."[2] Two centuries later, when Lenin came to power in Russia, he imposed a stifling censorship regime since "the bourgeois press is one of the most powerful weapons of the bourgeoisie" and "no less dangerous than bombs and machine-guns."[3]

In contemporary America, conservative and liberal universities alike are busy censoring "dangerous" or "hateful" ideas to "protect" students who apparently cannot—or should not—think for themselves (Arguments #2 and #3). Worry not that this is a novel anti–free speech argument. In 1231, Pope Gregory IX prescribed that unrepentant heretics pay "the debt of hatred," meaning death at the stake. The USSR's 1936 "Stalin" constitution declared punishable by law "any advocacy of racial or national exclusiveness or hatred and contempt."[4] Of course, any group that monopolizes power gets to define whose interests are protected by laws against "dangerous" or "hateful" ideas. South Africa's apartheid regime used the Jacobsen's Index of Objectionable Literature to ensure that nothing challenging white supremacy was published.[5]

Many on the left today believe free speech is just a veil for spreading conservative propaganda (Argument #6). They ought to recall a young Karl Marx's view that "the free press is the ubiquitous vigilant eye of a people's soul, the embodiment of a people's faith in itself."[6] Or the indefatigable British campaigner for universal suffrage and religious freedom, Richard Carlile, who spent a total of ten years in prison for "crimes" such as spreading the gospel of Thomas Paine's *The Age of Reason* to the lower classes in Britain's highly stratified society.[7]

Free expression only achieved its status as a universal human right (though one all too often honored in the breach) through a continuous struggle against the hydra-headed "10 arguments against"—which, like zombies, tend to rise from the grave, as soon as proponents of free speech think they have won for good.

Successfully mobilizing popular opinion against the "10 arguments against" demands a civic commitment to free speech rights beyond constitutional protections. This wisdom has been recognized by thinkers as diverse as John Stuart Mill, George Orwell, and Albert Einstein, and it could not be more relevant today. The Future of Free Speech's recent survey (conducted in October 2024) of thirty-three countries around the world found that, overall, people are more inclined to support government censorship of ideas they consider pernicious than in 2021.[8] This includes the United States, which dropped from 3rd to 9th in the ranking, with deeply worrying decreases in support for free speech among younger generations.

Two falsehoods contribute to slackening public support for free speech in the West specifically. The first is the widespread belief that there is no actual threat to speech today. The second is the belief that free expression should be subordinated to values considered more important, like social order and national security for conservatives or racial and economic justice in the eyes of American liberals.

In responding to the first falsehood, it is essential to place free speech in the global historical context. Western democracies no longer burn blasphemers at the stake, nor do they torture or execute political dissenters. Crucially, that is only the case because a robust culture of free speech forced the law to accommodate unpalatable expression. As recently as the 1950s in America, suspected communists and civil rights activists were arraigned for "sedition" or "treason." Only through a series of Supreme Court decisions in the twentieth century, culminating in the 1950s and 1960s, was the First Amendment's robust protection against content- and viewpoint-based restrictions securely entrenched.

The recent erosion of our free speech culture empowers the state to push legal boundaries. Witness the current administration's attempts to deport lawful permanent residents for expressing ideas with which it disagrees, or the previous administration's attempts to pressure social media platforms to remove speech it disfavored.

The culture of free speech has partly been eroded from within its traditional liberal heartland. Consider the argument in professor Mary Anne Franks's *Fearless Speech: Breaking Free from The First Amendment*—which has also been made by many other left-leaning academics, as well as journalists—that "First Amendment norms have consistently exalted and elevated reckless speech that benefits the powerful at the expense of the vulnerable [and] perpetuated and maintained a neo-Confederate ideology of white male supremacy."[9] This claim is entirely at odds with the history of the First Amendment and oblivious to many of its current beneficiaries.

In actuality, free speech is compatible with—indeed, essential for—liberal and conservative goals alike. Take the American independence movement—which many conservatives read as the triumph of their values of limited government against an oppressive English Crown. Defying British seditious libel laws was instrumental in this endeavor. As James Madison wrote, "to the press alone, chequered as it is with abuses . . . the United States owe much of the lights which conducted them to the rank of a free and independent nation." Had American presses been allowed to silence colonial dissent, might not the US remain as "miserable colonies, groaning under a foreign yoke?" Madison asked rhetorically.[10] And, of course, there also have been pious, traditionalist defenders of free speech rights. One of the eighteenth-century's most impassioned spokesmen for free speech, the Dutchman Elie Luzac, was a staunch Calvinist. So confident was he in his religious faith—as well as his faith in free speech and debate—that he declared, "we cannot take pride in the power of persuasion of the most important truths, as long as we prevent atheists, free-thinkers, and others of that ilk from brandishing their pen."[11]

Sadly, too many today—including government officials, university administrators and faculty, and even traditional-media leaders—have lost faith in free speech as the primary instrument for the pursuit of truth, and instead support the top-down imposition of ideological orthodoxy.

Free speech is the essential means to the end of any idea—conservative or liberal. Supporting free expression offers a chance to fact-check your views through debate—the "right to hear," as Strossen and Lukianoff point out, echoing Frederick Douglass in his timeless speech, "A Plea for Free Speech in Boston."

But there are even more "selfish" reasons for endorsing free speech. When you defend the right to speak freely, you are protecting your right to express *yourself* by agreeing to respect others' rights to do the same. It is the highest form of the Golden Rule: denying free speech rights to rivals only facilitates a crackdown on *your* ideas as soon as it is *their* turn in power. *The War On Words* makes a robust case for returning to that Golden Rule. Political leaders in Western democracies, and their citizens, should carefully read Strossen and Lukianoff's effective debunking of the "10 arguments against," lest they lose the very free speech culture that we all too often take for granted, to our own great peril.

Acknowledgments

The first thanks from both of us authors—Greg and Nadine—is to each other, for longstanding and fruitful collaboration on countless free speech matters, including on the blog posts for Greg's *Eternally Radical Idea* blog on FIRE's website, from which this book developed (we began the blog series in 2021). As a nice coincidence, at about the same time, each of us had independently undertaken to write out answers to the most common arguments we had constantly been encountering throughout our careers—arguments from scholars, politicians, and activists who supported various limits on free speech, and also from audience members in our constant public presentations. Even though our basic principles and ideas substantially overlap, we were fascinated to see that our answers nonetheless were substantially distinct from each other, so that each of us deepened our understandings as a result of reading the other's answers. Likewise, we hope that this book will be of interest even to readers who have significant knowledge about free speech issues, as well as to those with little or no background.

We encourage readers to visit our blog posts for answers to additional common arguments against free speech beyond those in this book, which we intentionally confined to what we considered the ten most important recurring arguments. Our blog posts can be found here: www.thefire.org/news/blogs/eternally-radical-idea/free-speech-does-not-equal-violence-part-1-answers-bad-arguments, as well as a suggested reading list included at www.thefire.org/research-learn/war-on-words.

We are both deeply grateful to Jacob Mchangama, whose unparalleled historical and global knowledge about free speech, as well as his unwavering commitment to free speech, illuminate his Foreword. We thank Jacob for his ongoing leadership in the international free speech movement and for his valued advice and advocacy as a FIRE Fellow alongside Nadine Strossen, other FIRE Fellows, and members of FIRE's Advisory Council, whom we additionally thank.

This book would not have been possible without the outstanding contributions—great in both quantity and quality—of many FIRE staff members. Adam Goldstein, FIRE's Vice President of Strategic Initiatives, served as principal researcher and editor. He deserves major credit not only for the endnotes, which are largely his work, but also for substantial contributions to the text itself. Nerida Brownlee, FIRE's Chief of Staff, served as the project manager and was superb in the role—overseeing every detail, keeping her gimlet eye on both the forest and the trees, and always bringing a rare and wonderful combination of efficiency and graciousness. Other FIRE staff members who made significant contributions (listed in alphabetical order) are Perry Fein (Executive Assistant to the President and CEO), Alisha Glennon (Chief Operating Officer), and Ryne Weiss (Director of Research) whose efforts shaped the 2021 blog posts, overseeing the editorial process and coordinating all contributions. Thanks also to Alex Morey and Jordan Howell for their superb editing skills and posting the individual essays. Special thanks are also due to FIRE's Communications team, including Nico Perrino (Executive Vice President), Matthew Harwood (Vice President of Communications), Daniel Burnett (Senior Director of Communications), and Tyler MacQueen (Director of Multimedia) for their skillful efforts in promoting this special book. Furthermore, we are grateful to FIRE's Board of Directors and Executive Leadership Team for their practical and institutional support throughout this book's development.

We thank Iona Italia for her early support, seeing the value of publishing Greg's 2021 article in *Areo Magazine*. That helped to spark first the blog posts and, ultimately, this book.

We sincerely thank Bernard Schweizer, Heresy Press's founder and director, for encouraging us to write this book and for his enthusiastic, effective engagement every step of the way. Heresy Press, as well as Skyhorse Publishing, of which it is an imprint, embody and promote the free speech principles to which we are both committed, at a time when too many in the publishing industry have failed to facilitate "freedom for the thought that we hate"—or, more specifically, for the thought that is hated by Twitter/X mobs and other cancel culture forces. As Justice Oliver Wendell Holmes declared when he penned that memorable phrase, it embodies the constitutional "principle . . . that more imperatively calls for attachment than any other." Yet that principle—along with free speech rights in general—cannot be realized without people who help to disseminate ideas and expression. Sadly, it takes courage to withstand cancel culture pressures, which have caused severe professional and personal harm to too many heterodox thinkers and their allies. Therefore, we gratefully acknowledge not only Bernard, but also Heresy Press's co-founder Liang Schweizer, and Skyhorse's President and Publisher, Tony Lyons.

Last but far from least, we thank the innumerable authors, audience members, co-panelists and sparring partners with whom we have discussed and debated free speech issues throughout our careers—who range all across the ideological spectrum—for their challenging questions and arguments. They have enabled us to honor the central teaching of John Stuart Mill's *On Liberty*: that we must always question every idea and belief, even—indeed, especially—those that we hold most dear. In short, the best way to fulfill the promise of freedom of speech is to ceaselessly question and argue about it.

Argument #1: Words Are Violence

Free speech was created under the false notion that words and violence are distinct, but we now know that certain speech is more akin to violence.

Nadine Strossen:

Physical violence directly and inevitably causes at least some physical harm, as well as associated psychic harm. Words may indeed have some harmful potential. Unlike physical violence, though, speech can influence listeners only through their intermediating perceptions, reactions, and actions, and only as one of countless other factors that also have potential influence. For this reason, hurling words at someone is materially different from hurling the proverbial "sticks and stones." Sticks and stones directly cause harm, through their own force, but words at most can potentially contribute to harm; whether particular words actually do cause harm depends on how individual listeners perceive and respond to them, which in turn is influenced by the listeners' personalities and circumstances, including innumerable other factors that also potentially influence their psyches and behavior.

When there is a sufficiently tight and direct causal nexus between speech and specific serious imminent harm, including violence, free speech principles permit such speech to be punished. For example, the government may punish a speaker who intentionally incites violence that is likely to happen imminently. As another example, under the "fighting words" doctrine, the government may punish a direct personal insult that is intended and likely to provoke an immediate violent reaction.[1]

"To this day, powerful critics of Black Lives Matter and other social justice activists seek to suppress and punish their expression on the ground that it allegedly constitutes or causes violence."

In contrast, when the government has been allowed to punish speech because of a more speculative, indirect connection between it and some potential future violence—as happened in the US in the past, and still occurs in other countries—the government predictably exercises this discretionary power to punish disempowered speakers and dissenting perspectives. After all, as Justice Oliver Wendell Holmes noted, "every idea is an incitement."[2] More recently, ACLU Legal Director David Cole observed that "A. Mitchell Palmer, J. Edgar Hoover, and Joseph McCarthy all used the advocacy of violence as a justification to punish people who associated with Communists, socialists, or civil rights groups."[3] To this day, powerful critics of Black Lives Matter and other social justice activists seek to suppress and punish their expression on the ground that it allegedly constitutes or causes violence.

Greg Lukianoff:

Speech equals violence isn't a new idea. It's a very old—and very bad—idea.

The whole point of freedom of speech, from its beginning, has been to enable people to sort things out *without* resorting to violence. A quotation often attributed to Sigmund Freud (which he attributed to another writer) conveys this: "The first human being who hurled an insult instead of a stone was the founder of civilization."[4]

On campus, I often run into people—not only students, but professors—who seem to think they're the first to notice that the distinction between what we deem to be appropriate responses to speech and violence, respectively, is a social construct; in other words, this distinction has meaning only because we collectively decide it should. Those who stress that this distinction is a social construct then conclude that this makes the distinction arbitrary, so that they can draw the line where they please.

Yes, a strong distinction between how we legitimately respond to harm caused by speech versus how we respond to it as a result of violence is a comparatively recent social construct, but it's one of the best social constructs for peaceful coexistence, innovation, and progress that's ever been invented. Drawing a line between acceptable responses to speech and violence also creates a very simple rule to follow, in practice. Under the *speech equals violence* philosophy, *my* speech—even if sharp, brutal, and filled with invective—is still simply speech. Indeed, it might be commendable, righteous rage. But my opponent's speech, even if it's similarly sharp and brutal, is violence—and I am therefore allowed to respond with violence. This argument was made in an attempt to justify the violent response to conservative provocateur Milo Yiannopoulos's 2017 speech at UC Berkeley, [5] where the campus free speech movement had been born. The student newspaper published article after article arguing that Milo's hate speech demanded violent retaliation.[6]

That same year, Northeastern University psychology professor and author Lisa Feldman Barrett penned an op-ed in the *New York Times* arguing that because words and violence can each cause a stress response, there's no clear delineation between them. [7] But many things in life induce a stress response. If a stress response is all that is required to equate speech with violence, thus justifying a violent reaction, then every dad who punched the referee at his nine-year-old's soccer game is a hero.

That is the endgame of *speech is violence:* it makes actual violence inevitable. It is a formula for a chain reaction of endless violence, repression, and regression.[8]

Argument #2: Words Are Dangerous

Free speech rests on the faulty notion that words are harmless.

Nadine Strossen:

To the contrary, speech is protected precisely because of its powerful potential to affect hearts, minds, and actions; that power may contribute to either good or harm, depending on countless contextual factors. Let me cite a vivid example from recent US history: the virulently racist "Unite the Right" ralliers' chants in Charlottesville, Virginia in 2017. This expression no doubt caused at least some observers to adopt or harden racist attitudes, and to engage in racially discriminatory actions, including violence. Equally undoubtedly, it caused other observers to repudiate racism and to engage in anti-racist activism.

> "Experience also demonstrates that censorship is only a superficial 'quick fix' for the actual problems it allegedly addresses."

US law already permits the government to punish speech that, considered in its overall context, directly or imminently causes certain serious harm—consistent with what is sometimes called the "emergency test," referring to a famous opinion by Justice Brandeis, declaring that "only an emergency can justify repression."[1] So the pertinent question is whether the government should be granted more latitude to punish speech that doesn't pose an emergency—when it has only an indirect, attenuated connection to potential future harm. To be sure, such speech may well contribute to harm. However, to justify expanding government power to impose non-emergency speech restrictions, we would logically have to examine the following additional factors about such additional speech restrictions:

1. Would they actually, materially reduce speech's harmful potential?
2. Or might they instead be counter-productive–for example, by increasing attention to and sympathy for the speech?
3. Are there non-censorial alternative measures, which could be at least as effective in reducing the speech's harmful potential? For example, education?

Experience throughout history and around the world demonstrates that government discretion to punish speech because of its indirect harmful potential constitutes a license to punish views and speakers that the government disfavors. Prior to the Supreme Court's adoption of the speech-protective emergency principle in the second half of the twentieth century, government regularly suppressed the speech of crusaders for various causes that contemporaries viewed as dangerous and harmful, including: abolition,[2] women's suffrage,[3] opposition to wars and the draft,[4] labor unions,[5] Communism,[6] socialism,[7] civil rights,[8] reproductive freedom,[9] and LGBTQ+ rights.[10]

Experience also demonstrates that censorship is only a superficial "quick fix" for the actual problems it allegedly addresses. Meaningful approaches require addressing underlying attitudes and actual actions. For example, far more effective than outlawing "hate speech" is educating people to reject discriminatory ideas and punishing discriminatory conduct.

Greg Lukianoff:

If free speech were not powerful, there would be no need either to protect it OR to ban it. It's not surprising that free speech can be harsh, since it's meant as a replacement for *actual violence*!

Historically, freedom of speech has been justified as part of a system for resolving disputes without resorting to actual violence. Acceptance of freedom of speech is a way to live with genuine conflict among points of view (which has *always* existed) without resorting to coercive force.

I've made this point many times in my career, in many different ways, but the most popular online is the way I once put it during a 2009 appearance on John Stossel's eponymous TV show:

> Words are supposed to hurt. That's considered a legitimate way of fighting things out. And what did [speech] replace in the historical scene? It replaced actual violence. Words are supposed to be free so we CAN actually fight things out, in the battleplace of ideas, so we don't end up fighting them out in civil wars.
>
> If we try to . . . ban anything that can hurt someone's feelings, everyone is reduced to silence.

It's not surprising that free speech in a democracy can be very heated, when that protection covers people's most sincerely held religious beliefs and their opinions about matters of life and death.

As I put this in my first book, *Unlearning Liberty*:

> The idea that we should campaign against hurtful speech among adults arises from a failure to understand that free speech is our chosen method of resolving disagreements, using words rather than weapons. Open debate is our enlightened means of determining nothing less than how we order our society, what is true and what is false, what wars we should fight, what policies we should pass, whom we should put behind bars for the rest of their lives, and who gets to control our government. This is a deadly serious business.[11]

Being a citizen in a democratic republic is supposed to be challenging; it's supposed to ask something of its citizens. It requires a certain minimal toughness—and commitment to self-governing—to become informed about difficult issues and to argue, organize, and vote accordingly. As the Supreme Court observed in 1949, in *Terminiello v Chicago*, speech "may indeed best serve its high purpose when it induces a condition of unrest, creates dissatisfaction with conditions as they are, or even stirs people to anger."[12]

The only model that asks nothing of its citizens in terms of learning, autonomy, and decision-making is the authoritarian one. By arguing that freedom *from* speech is often more important than freedom *of* speech,[13] advocates unwittingly embrace the nineteenth-century (anti-)speech justification for czarist power: the idea that the Russian peasant has the best kind of freedom, the freedom from the burden of freedom[14] itself (because it surely is a burden).[15]

Argument #3: Hate Speech Isn't Free Speech

Hate speech laws are important for reducing intolerance, even if there may be some examples of abuse.

Nadine Strossen:

Hate speech laws, though often well-intentioned, are inherently vague, prone to misuse by those in power, and less effective than counterspeech.[1]

US free speech law does allow government to restrict "hate speech"—a term that has no specific legal meaning, but generally refers to speech conveying hateful, discriminatory ideas—in appropriately limited circumstances: when the speech, considered in its overall context, directly causes or imminently threatens certain serious harms, such as targeted threats or harassment or intentional incitement of imminent violence.[2] However, US free speech law appropriately bars government from restricting hate speech solely because of disagreement with or disapproval of a speaker's viewpoint, or because of vague fears that the speech might indirectly lead to some potential harm at some future time.

> "One person's cherished repudiation of intolerance is someone else's hate speech."

Prior to the 1960s, US law did give government broader discretionary power to punish hate speech, and the laws in many other countries continue to do so. (I will use the term "hate speech laws" to refer to these kinds of measures.) These laws are often intended to promote important, positive goals, such as reducing intolerance. In practice, though, the laws are at best ineffective, and at worst counterproductive, in actually advancing those goals. For this reason, many human rights activists, all over the world, have opposed hate speech laws, noting that they too often are used to silence speakers who oppose government policies or advocate minority group rights—even in modern democratic countries.[3]

It is important to understand that hate speech laws are inherently likely to be enforced in ways that further entrench dominant political and societal groups, and that further disempower marginalized individuals and groups. This pattern is not a result of occasional "abuses" of the laws, but rather is the inevitable, systematic result of any use of such laws, given their irreducible vagueness. Just consider the wide-ranging and even contradictory uses of the epithet "hate speech" in current US political debates. For example, some powerful politicians denounce Black Lives Matter advocacy as hate speech,[4] whereas others in turn denounce that very denunciation as hate speech.[5] One person's cherished repudiation of intolerance is someone else's hate speech.

No matter how many synonyms are invoked to try to circumscribe the inherently vague, broad, and manipulable concept of "hate," these laws unavoidably vest broad discretion in enforcing authorities, consistently resulting in enforcement patterns that are arbitrary at best, discriminatory at worst.[6] Even when such authorities act in utmost good faith, they cannot enforce such unduly vague laws except in accordance with their own subjective values, or those of other people. As one would expect in a government where officials are (appropriately) accountable to their constituents, officials are likely to enforce these open-textured laws in accordance with the values of powerful community interest groups.

> "Hate speech laws are inherently likely to be enforced in ways that further entrench dominant political and societal groups, and that further disempower marginalized individuals and groups."

Even when hate speech laws are enforced to punish speech of avowed racists, they are not effective in reducing intolerance. There is no correlation between the enforcement of hate speech laws and the reduction of intolerance. For example, both during the Weimar Republic (1918–33) and in recent decades, Germany has enforced strict hate speech laws. Yet Hitler and his Nazi party rose to power during the Weimar period, and today's explicitly racist AfD party has grown dramatically in the recent past. Both periods saw disturbing upsurges in violence against Jews and other minority groups (see Argument #10 about the Holocaust).

In the US, although much progress remains to be made in reducing intolerance, much already has been made since the days of Jim Crow. Yet the constitutionality of hate speech laws was not called into question until the 1960s. In other words, the reduction in intolerance accompanied the reduction in government power to suppress hate speech—not the opposite. In fact, civil rights leaders and historians alike concur that robust speech protection—extending even to hate speech—was necessary for promoting the racial justice cause; local officials routinely wielded any speech-restrictive laws to stifle civil rights advocacy. As the civil rights icon John Lewis famously proclaimed: "Without freedom of speech and the right to dissent, the Civil Rights movement would have been a bird without wings."[7]

Again, it is important to understand why the foregoing patterns are not merely coincidental, or the result of occasional "abuses" of hate speech laws. Rather, such laws' inherent features doom them to inefficacy in combating intolerance.

Logically, hate speech laws leave three options for those inclined to engage in the targeted speech, all of which have negative consequences for reducing intolerance: Some hate speech will be driven underground, thus reducing opportunities for discovering and dissuading those who purvey or heed it; some hate speech will be camouflaged in more subtle rhetoric to evade punishment, thereby making the speech more appealing to a broader audience; and some will remain unchanged, or perhaps even ramped up, as the speakers seek the publicity that results from suppression efforts.

Committed racists and their supporters are not likely to repudiate their beliefs in response to censorship or punishment, but to the contrary may well become more resentful and hardened in their attitudes. Moreover, attempts to suppress their ideas inevitably draw more attention to those ideas. This phenomenon is so common that there are multiple terms for it, including "the Streisand effect," which refers to an effort by famed performer Barbra Streisand to suppress online photographs of her Malibu beach house, which had exactly the opposite effect—dramatically increasing the number of people who viewed the photographs.[8] The added attention to speech that is targeted under hate speech laws leads to increased sympathy from some quarters, including from those who view the speakers as free speech martyrs. For these reasons, many hatemongers welcome attempted or actual censorship. Far from muting their ideas, such efforts amplify them. For these same reasons, experts in combatting intolerance oppose efforts to suppress white supremacist speakers or rallies. They explain that such suppressive efforts might feel morally satisfying, but they are strategically counterproductive, giving hatemongers the very attention they crave.[9]

While censorship is an ineffective means to reduce intolerance, non-censorial strategies have shown much more promise in doing so. The term "counterspeech" is often used to describe any speech that counters the ideas and attitudes reflected in hate speech. It can take countless forms and be tailored to myriad particular contexts and purposes, including, for example: proactive education that instills values of tolerance and support for equal human rights for all; responsive information and analysis to refute advocacy of discriminatory policies; and supportive communications to individuals who have been disparaged by hate speech.

Contrary to common misconceptions, counterspeech should not be the responsibility of individuals or groups who are targeted by hate speech. Nor should counterspeech be limited to defensive responses to hate speech. Rather, all of us who are committed to countering hatred and discrimination should seize every opportunity to proactively advocate tolerance and related values, including equality, dignity, diversity, and inclusion.

Many self-described "formers"—former members and even leaders of groups espousing hateful doctrines—have been "redeemed" (as they refer to it) as a result of exchanges with others, who reach out to them with compassion and empathy, helping the "formers" wean themselves away from their hateful ideologies. Such "redeemed" individuals consistently attest that treating them in a punitive or stigmatizing way, in contrast, only has an alienating impact.[10] This experience aligns with the increasing support for "restorative justice" as a more constructive approach to addressing any anti-social conduct than the harshly punitive approach our criminal legal system has traditionally pursued.

Multiple reports by human rights activists in many countries and in international agencies have concluded that counterspeech should be prioritized over censorship. Even though hate speech laws are permitted in these other countries, human rights experts have concluded that counterspeech is preferable from a pragmatic perspective. For example, the European Commission against Racism and Intolerance, which monitors the implementation of the many European hate speech laws, concluded that, in contrast with such laws, counterspeech is "much more likely to prove effective" in curbing intolerance.[11]

Greg Lukianoff:

Hate speech laws (and their American cousin, bias response hotlines) have been arbitrarily enforced and have contributed to greater polarization and suppression of dissent. Since the widespread passage of hate speech codes in Europe, religious and ethnic intolerance there has gone up. During the same period, ethnic and religious tolerance has improved in the United States. At least a dozen Western European countries have hate speech laws, many of which run counter to their legal or historical commitments to free speech. But even though those laws have been on the books for years, by most measures Western Europe is less tolerant than the US. Western Europe as a whole scores 17 percent on the antisemitism index, meaning about 17 percent of the population harbors antisemitic attitudes—even though many of their hate speech laws explicitly prohibit Holocaust denial.[12] France passed its Gayssot Act outlawing Holocaust denial in 1990, yet as recently as January 2025 it held a 13 percent antisemitism index score.[13] In the US, with no such laws, the antisemitism index is ranked at 9 percent.[14]

"Censorship doesn't generally change people's opinions, but it does make them more likely to talk only to those with whom they already agree."

Nor has restricting hate speech prevented the spread of other forms of intolerance, beyond antisemitism. In 1986, the UK passed a law against "words or behaviour . . . likely to stir up racial hatred"[15]; yet, in the 1990s, racial tolerance decreased.[16] Despite having repeatedly expanded its hate speech laws since 1994,[17] Germany has been experiencing increased Islamophobia and anti-Semitism.[18]

Cracking down on hate speech has not only failed to decrease intolerance; worse yet, there are solid grounds to believe that cracking down on hate speech has helped to *increase* intolerance. After all, censorship doesn't generally change people's opinions, but it does make them more likely to talk only to those with whom they already agree. And what happens when people only talk to politically similar people? The well-documented effect of group/political polarization takes over, and the speaker—who may have moderated her belief when exposed to dissenting opinions—becomes more radicalized in the direction of her hatred.[19]

Hate speech laws are the worst of both worlds. While they do not reduce intolerance, they do suppress important expression. For example, criminal charges that target allegedly "hateful" ideas or expression have repeatedly been brought against protesters and journalists, in the US and abroad.

In the US, hate speech is constitutionally protected (unless it satisfies one of the context-defined criteria for unprotected expression, such as punishable threats or harassment), but crimes such as assault or vandalism may be prosecuted as "hate crimes" or "bias crimes" and subject to enhanced punishment if the victim was intentionally singled out for a discriminatory reason.[20] While the US laws against hate crimes thus notably differ from other countries' laws against hate speech, all such laws are united in predictably being weaponized against whatever expression or speakers the authorities disfavor. Both hate crime and hate speech charges target legitimate expression and newsgathering by protesters and journalists, in the US and other countries:

- In 2023, a Black Lives Matter activist in Calgary, Canada was charged with a hate crime for allegedly blocking access to a Catholic school; the activist said a police officer had taken her phone during a protest and she was trying to get it back.[21] The charge was later dropped and the Calgary Police Service called it a "clerical error."[22]
- In June 2024, a woman in Buckinghamshire, England was charged with a "racially aggravated public order offence" for holding up a sign at a protest that depicted MP Suella Braverman and then-Prime Minister Rishi Sunak as coconuts (implying that they're brown on the outside, white on the inside).[23] She was later acquitted.
- In August 2024, New York City police charged independent videographer Samuel Seligson with felony hate crimes after raiding his home twice.[24]

> The charges were related to Seligson's following a group of pro-Palestinian protesters as they smeared red paint and hung banners at the apartments of the Brooklyn Museum's Jewish president and director. Seligson had been arrested in May for covering another pro-Palestinian protest; those charges were later dropped.[25]

A troubling development going forward is the adoption of university-style "bias response hotlines" by local and state governments. These phone lines permit anyone who feels "targeted" by speech or expression to make a report to the state that will be kept on file and potentially used by the government to "keep an eye" on people. According to journalist Aaron Sibarium, "by the end of 2025, nearly 100 million Americans will live in a state where they can be reported for protected speech."[26]

Sibarium called Oregon's hotline to report a fictional "bias incident," which consisted of seeing someone flying an Israeli flag. The hotline, run by the state's Department of Justice, accepted the report.[27] Connecticut, Maryland, California, Illinois, and New York all already have hotlines.[28]

Bias response hotlines originated in higher education—where they have done much more harm than good. And the reported "bias incidents" were often trivial. The *Wall Street Journal* told the stories of (among others) a student reported for watching a Ben Shapiro video, a professor reported for defending then-Judge Brett Kavanaugh's nomination to the Supreme Court, and a faculty member reported for giving a "rude look" to a trans person.[29]

The fact that these calls are non-adversarial means that the person being accused never even knows of the accusation let alone has a chance to respond, even though a report is being made accusing them of, potentially, hateful behavior. (Assuming the accused person even exists, which, as Sibarium's reporting illustrates, is entirely optional.) For those reports to be collected and aggregated over time creates a tool that could easily be used to target ideological opponents in the same way that "false-flagging" social media posts is used today.[30] Even if someone found out about an accusation made to a bias response hotline, there isn't usually a method of challenging it.

Then there's the issue of mission creep. In the college context, a 2017 study by the University of North Carolina-Charlotte interviewed twenty-one administrators at nineteen universities to better understand how they saw the role of Bias Response Team members.[31] Among the responses were some flatly unconstitutional statements, such as the purpose of the team was to step in "when the exercise of individual rights becomes reckless and irresponsible" and that "hate speech we don't allow, but free speech we do."[32]

Accusations of hate speech, hate crime for protesting or newsgathering, and bias response hotlines all have the same effect on observers: we become more careful, and less free, about what we say. A free speech culture shouldn't tolerate any of them.

Argument #4: About Shoutdowns

Shoutdowns are an exercise of speech rights, not censorship.

Note: This answer refers to and assumes situations where audience members have attempted to shout down events and keep them from proceeding, as opposed to brief heckling that is itself protected speech.

Nadine Strossen:

Protesters who have disrupted speakers through loud, persistent shouting have argued that such tactics, far from *violating* freedom of speech, constitute *exercises* of such freedom.

To be sure, these tactics convey messages—namely, disagreement with the suppressed ideas, and also rejection of the notion that the speaker and audience should have a right to convey and receive these ideas. Yet the Supreme Court rightly has recognized that the sole fact that conduct conveys a message is not enough for it to be treated as "speech" within the First Amendment's ambit, let alone as speech that is immune from regulation or punishment. Were it otherwise, there would be a First Amendment defense to even the most heinous, harmful violent crimes, including the assassination of a political leader; after all, such assassinations surely convey the murderers' abhorrence of the victims' policies.

Ironically, many who assert this expansive concept of protected free speech when they defend speech-suppressive tactics such as shoutdowns assert a much narrower concept concerning the suppressed speech itself. Critics of the targeted speech often proclaim that the speech is "violence," which has no claim to First Amendment protection (see Argument #1). Most ironically, some who attack disfavored words as "violence" defend actual physical violence against those who utter such words. Alarmingly, recent surveys indicate that substantial percentages of college students condone physical violence against controversial speakers.[1]

What are the actual First Amendment rights and wrongs in these situations?

First, some conduct is sufficiently expressive to be eligible for First Amendment protection. Classic examples include burning a US flag in political protest and marching in a demonstration. To come within the First Amendment's scope, conduct must either be inherently expressive—for example, a parade—or it must be intended to convey "a particularized message" and have a "great" likelihood that "the message would be understood by those who viewed it."[2] Even conduct that meets these standards may still be regulated, so long as the regulation focuses on the general conduct, rather than its associated message, and promotes an important public purpose. Accordingly, even if we assumed—purely hypothetically—that a physical assault on a speaker would trigger First Amendment analysis, the assailant nevertheless could—and should—still be punished, to further the important public interest in physical safety.

What about speech-suppressive tactics that primarily consist of words, and hence are clearly eligible for First Amendment protection? The most common such tactic is shouting down the speaker, making it impossible for the audience to hear the speaker's words.

The First Amendment clearly protects protesters who express their disagreement with a speaker's message in a peaceful, non-disruptive manner, which does not substantially interfere with the speaker's right to speak or the audience's right to listen. Permissible non-disruptive protest tactics include: holding signs with messages (so long as the signs do not block the audience's view of the speaker); handing out leaflets; wearing T-shirts or other apparel with messages; walking out of the venue after the speaker is introduced or begins to speak; occasional brief and relatively quiet hissing and booing during the speaker's presentation; and even occasional loud but short bursts of expression conveying disapproval of the speaker's statements. In contrast, impermissible disruptive protest tactics substantially interfere with the speaker's efforts to communicate to the audience—for example, through sustained shouting.

> "Government may . . . prohibit and punish any conduct, including shouting, that interferes with speakers' and audience members' exercise of their First Amendment rights."

In some situations, reasonable people can disagree about whether protests have crossed the line between non-disruptive and disruptive tactics. This is the case, for example, if protests solely delay an event, or temporarily interfere with the speaker's delivery of a message, rather than completely halting the event. In many recent situations, the protesters clearly do aim to completely halt the event, and succeed in doing so—either by shouting so persistently that the speaker gives up trying to talk, or by threatening physical violence against the speaker or others, thus prompting campus officials to cancel the event due to security concerns.

In accordance with general, sensible First Amendment principles, the government may impose "viewpoint-neutral" restrictions on any verbal disruption tactics. Such restrictions do not single out the speech's particular viewpoint or messages, but rather, they regulate the speech's "time, place, or manner." For example, all expression during a speaker's presentation could be limited to particular locations, durations, or decibel levels, to prevent undue interference with the speaker's message. The First Amendment permits such viewpoint-neutral regulations so long as they promote an important public purpose and leave "ample alternative channels" for the regulated expression to reach its intended audience. The protection of First Amendment rights is indisputably a sufficiently important purpose, and protesters have "ample" non-disruptive means to convey their objections to speakers and audience members. Therefore, government may—and should—prohibit and punish any conduct, including shouting, that interferes with speakers' and audience members' exercise of their First Amendment rights.

The term "heckler's veto" has been used to describe the impact that disruptive protesters have on others' free speech rights when the protesters' speech (and other disruptive conduct) is not punished. In effect, the "hecklers"—those who disagree with a speaker's message—are given veto power over the First Amendment freedoms of speakers *and* audience members. Because heckler's vetoes are likely to be exercised by individuals and groups who wield power in particular communities, they predictably tend to target relatively powerless, unpopular speakers and groups in those communities.

The term was coined by University of Chicago Law Professor Harry Kalven, in his classic 1965 book about the essential role that robust free speech rights played in the civil rights movement, *The Negro and the First Amendment.* In that historic context, hostile mobs too often sought to exercise a heckler's veto to silence pro-civil rights advocates, and law enforcement officials too often failed to punish the mob.

A 1951 case, which the Supreme Court effectively overturned in 1963, illustrates this general pattern. In *Feiner v. New York*, the majority opinion allowed a heckler's veto, over spirited dissents by liberal Justices Black and Douglas.[3] Irving Feiner, "a young college student," was speaking at an open-air meeting in Syracuse, New York on behalf of "The Young Progressives" organization, to "a crowd of about seventy-five or eighty people, both Negro and white." The Court's majority opined that one of Feiner's statements triggered hostile demonstrators' disruption and hence (assertedly) justified police officers' demand that he cease speaking. According to the majority, Feiner "gave the impression that he was endeavoring to arouse the Negro people against the whites" when he said that black people "don't have equal rights, and they should rise up in arms and fight for them." As Justice Black noted in dissent, this ruling meant that, "as a practical matter, minority speakers can be silenced in any city." Notably, the Court's 1963 decision invalidating *Feiner*—along with so many of the Court's leading free speech cases—was in a case upholding the rights of peaceful protesters during the Civil Rights Movement.[4]

On today's campuses, the hecklers are often following in Irving Feiner's footsteps, insofar as they espouse progressive causes and castigate the denial of equal rights to black Americans. Yet, too many of today's progressive students also follow in the footsteps of Feiner's hecklers and censors, insofar as they seek to stifle views of which they disapprove. And too often campus officials follow in the footsteps of the officials who facilitated the silencing of Feiner: They fail to punish the hecklers and to protect the speakers and audience members. Paraphrasing Justice Black, today's heckler's vetoes "can silence" speakers espousing "minority" views "in any [campus community]."[5] Indeed, heckler's vetoes have been deployed against liberal speakers on campus by conservative protesters, as well as against conservative speakers by liberal protesters.[6]

The historic record of heckler's vetoes, and their continued power to suppress marginalized voices and views, should give pause to anyone who might be tempted to defend this tactic as potentially promoting any progressive cause.

Greg Lukianoff:

Shouting down a speaker to stop an event from proceeding is mob censorship, full stop.

This argument was all over X in 2022 following incidents where members of the audience shouted down speakers at UNT,[7] UC Hastings,[8] and Yale.[9] It was bad then and it's bad now. It gives the shouters the power to dictate what anyone else is able to say or to hear. The idea that a group—or even a single individual pulling a fire alarm[10] or banging a cowbell[11]—can decide what others can and cannot listen to is incompatible with pluralism. It replaces the free exchange of ideas with a system of "might makes right," and it is especially egregious for this to happen in the university context where the free exchange of ideas and the freedom to seek out any information is most important.

This is so obvious that, I believe, those who make this argument either do so in bad faith, or have not thought through the implications of this position. For example, no one would argue that one has a right to go to a university orchestra concert and play electrically amplified guitar from their seat. It is equally hard to imagine that those sympathetic to shout-downs of conservative speakers at Yale and Hastings would make the same argument if, for example, a pro-choice speaker was shut down by rowdy pro-life protestors, or if a student shouted down his professor for the duration of class. And yet these examples logically follow from the asserted free speech "right" for some audience members to take over an event.

"The university is meant to be a place of uniquely open minds, where ideas—even wrong and offensive ones—are interrogated."

In each of these cases, a government official or university administrator stepping in to stop the individual or mob from dictating what can be said reflects a positive duty to protect freedom of speech. The university is meant to be a place of uniquely open minds, where ideas—even wrong and offensive ones—are interrogated. Eventually, by way of the '*via negativa*' principle (in other words, by subtracting what does not belong), we get closer to the truth, even if we never reach it.

This process is short-circuited when some—through shouting, noisemakers, or fire alarms—prevent others from speaking and being heard by those who wish to hear them. Those who shut down events through disruption don't just deprive listeners who agree with the speaker from hearing speech; they also deprive those who disagree and want to interrogate the viewpoint with pointed questions, and those who want to listen with scholarly detachment to learn more about the view being expressed.

It's especially galling for this to occur at a law school—the work of lawyers requires being able to argue effectively against opposing viewpoints. And responding effectively to opposing viewpoints first requires *hearing them out.*

The important First Amendment right to receive information and ideas, which the Supreme Court long has recognized,[12] was well explained by Justice Thurgood Marshall in a 1972 opinion:[13]

> The right to speak and hear–including the right to inform others and to be informed about public issues–are inextricably part of that process. The freedom to speak and the freedom to hear are inseparable; they are two sides of the same coin. But the coin itself is the process of thought and discussion. The activity of speakers becoming listeners and listeners becoming speakers in the vital interchange of thought is the "means indispensable to the discovery and spread of political truth."

Long before the Supreme Court championed the right to hear, Frederick Douglass did so after an abolitionist event he organized in Boston in 1860 was shouted down by outraged members of the public:[14]

> There can be no right of speech where any man, however lifted up, or however humble, however young, or however old, is overawed by force, and compelled to suppress his honest sentiments. Equally clear is the right to hear. To suppress free speech is a double wrong. It violates the rights of the hearer as well as those of the speaker. It is just as criminal to rob a man of his right to speak and hear as it would be to rob him of his money.

If you are not persuaded by these philosophical arguments, here is a pragmatic one: If we continue down the path of allowing anyone with the ability to draw a big enough crowd to shut down any speech they do not like, it will have dire consequences for speech that you like. Whatever your political leanings, a shout-down opposing them has almost certainly occurred at some point.[15] Normalizing this behavior and allowing it to go unpunished will incentivize more of it: There will always be parts of the country where it will be easier to assemble a mob opposed to your views than in favor of them.

As evidence indicates, these shout-downs are often allowed to proceed, go unpunished, or even receive encouragement from administrators because some administrators dislike the particular speech being shouted down.[16] But the bottom line is this: A university that allows—or disallows—speech based on the assumption that "might makes right" is one where speech isn't really free at all.

Argument #5: Free Speech Is Outdated

The arguments for freedom of speech are outdated in the age of the internet; it's time for new thinking.

Nadine Strossen:

Far from being "an outdated idea," free speech is instead a timeless idea, which has withstood constant counterarguments and repressive efforts, throughout history and around the world.

Freedom of speech has repeatedly been championed by succeeding new generations, in every kind of political system, and in every culture. It is protected in the constitutions and other governing charters of countries worldwide, including those most recently adopted.[1] Freedom of speech is also enshrined as a fundamental, universal human right in the Universal Declaration of Human Rights[2] as well as the International Covenant on Civil and Political Rights, to which a full 178 countries are parties out of the 193 UN member states.[3] Furthermore, freedom of speech is enshrined in the foundational regional human rights treaties for Europe,[4] the Americas,[5] and Africa[6] (there is no comparable Asia-wide treaty). Notably, even governments that do not protect free speech in practice nonetheless feel the need to profess fidelity to it, in an effort to attain legitimacy in the eyes of the world, as well as their own citizens.

Also noteworthy—as well as inspiring and heartbreaking—is how many courageous human rights activists are willing to risk their safety and even lives for freedom of speech. In 1989, Iran's Supreme Leader Ayatollah Khomeini issued a fatwa (an official Islamic law ruling) against author Salman Rushdie, decrying Rushdie's 1988 novel *The Satanic Verses* as assertedly "written, edited, and published against Islam."[7] The fatwa was accompanied by a large bounty to anyone who assassinated Rushdie, thus forcing him to go into hiding for nine years, before courageously deciding to face the ongoing risks of living freely—resulting in a brutal 2022 knife attack that almost killed him and left him severely injured.[8] Rushdie memorably responded to those who questioned the importance of the free speech that had jeopardized and severely constrained his life: "Free speech is the whole thing, the whole ball game. Free speech is life itself."[9]

More recently, speaking from his prison cell upon receiving the Nobel Peace Prize in 2010, Chinese human rights activist Liu Xiaobo eloquently described this precious freedom, for which he had sacrificed his physical liberty: "Free expression is the foundation of human rights, the source of humanity, and the mother of truth."[10]

The arguments both for and against freedom of speech continue to involve the same eternal, fundamental issues of principle that have been debated worldwide throughout history: why free speech is important, and how to draw the appropriate line between protected and punishable speech. For one compelling account, see Jacob Mchangama's book: *Free Speech: A History from Socrates to Social Media.*[11] Ironically, one of the consistently recurring issues concerns the regularly repeated claim that changed societal circumstances—in particular, new communications technologies—have made established free speech principles obsolete.

To be sure, changing factual developments are pertinent in evaluating how free speech principles should be enforced in particular circumstances. Whether certain speech directly threatens imminent, serious harm that can't be averted without restricting the speech—hence justifying its restriction under modern free speech principles—depends on the factual details surrounding the speech. For example, new technology may facilitate "deepfakes" that could be restricted as defamation or fraud, whereas such restrictions might not be warranted for less sophisticated false communications, because deepfakes are more likely to mislead reasonable viewers.

In contrast with the changing factual circumstances to which free speech principles and rationales are applied, what is the basis for claiming that these underlying principles or rationales themselves should be changed?

Experience around the world and throughout history demonstrates that when a government has been granted more discretion to restrict speech than under the current First Amendment speech-protective principles, it predictably wields that discretion disproportionately to the disadvantage of minority views and voices. Accordingly, far from being outdated, the current principles are more important now than ever, so that traditionally marginalized people and perspectives are vigorously protected. The recent surge in social justice activism—along with all other movements for greater equality and inclusivity throughout history—has depended on robust free speech, and would be impeded by rollbacks of such freedom based on the claim that it is somehow "outdated."

Just as modern speech-protective principles stand the

test of time, the same is true of the classic rationales for free speech, which recognize its crucial and enduring role in promoting essential goals, including the search for truth, democratic self-government, and individual autonomy. Surely these goals themselves are not outdated, nor is the reason for preferring free speech to censorship (beyond the limited circumstances in which contemporary speech-protective principles permit speech to be restricted) as a vehicle for pursuing them: free speech will not necessarily secure such goals, but censorship will necessarily undermine them.

Those who criticize freedom of speech correctly note that it does not guarantee that truth will ultimately prevail in the proverbial "marketplace of ideas" (see Argument #7, about this marketplace metaphor). What such critics generally fail to note, however, is what censorship does guarantee about the search for truth: under a censorial regime, any truth that challenges government policies or officials is especially unlikely to prevail. Historically, governments have wielded censorship power precisely as one would expect: to suppress speakers who dissent from current orthodoxy and advocate reform—from abolitionists through Black Lives Matter activists. This pattern, which constitutes an important reason to support freedom of speech, is no more "outdated" than any other pro-speech rationales. For example, all over the country, BLM protesters,[12] as well as journalists who cover them[13] and legal observers who seek to protect their rights,[14] have been subject to unwarranted suppression. No wonder so many leading crusaders for racial justice and other human rights causes have celebrated free speech and decried censorship.

"It is the anti-free-speech arguments that are outdated. Those arguments are not only outdated today; they have been wrong every one of the many times they have been made throughout history, including in response to every new communications technology, dating back to the printing press."

Likewise, it is hard to fathom what reason could support the claim that free speech's essential role in facilitating democracy is somehow "outdated." As the Supreme Court declared, freedom of speech about public affairs entails "more than self-expression; it is the essence of self-government."[15] Even though freedom of speech shields some expression, such as disinformation, which may adversely impact our democracy, government censorship of such speech (beyond the strictly limited categories of false statements that are now punishable) is diametrically antithetical to democratic values. As the Supreme Court explained in a 2000 decision: "The Constitution exists precisely so that . . . judgments [about debatable matters] . . . can be formed, tested, and expressed. . . . These judgments are for the individual to make, not for the Government to decree, even with the mandate or approval of a majority."[16]

Finally, it is difficult to imagine why freedom of speech might even arguably be outdated as a means to promote individual autonomy. Echoing esteemed philosophers, the Supreme Court repeatedly has recognized that free speech has intrinsic value as an essential prerequisite for individual self-actualization, in addition to its key instrumental roles in promoting truth and self-government. As the Supreme Court stated in a 2000 decision, "the right to think is the beginning of freedom, and speech must be protected from the government because speech is the beginning of thought."[17]

In sum, for all its shortcomings and risks, freedom of speech is far more effective than censorship in advancing truth, democracy, and individual autonomy—not to mention all other human rights. It is the anti-free-speech arguments that are outdated. Those arguments are not only outdated today; they have been wrong every one of the many times they have been made throughout history, including in response to every new communications technology, dating back to the printing press.

Greg Lukianoff:

First of all, censorship is a very old idea, as old as our species; a shared cultural value of free speech is comparatively the "new kid on the block." As Nat Hentoff once wrote, quoting former *Los Angeles Times* editor Phil Kerby, "censorship is the strongest drive in human nature; sex is a weak second."[18] You can see arguments justifying censorship going back as far as written records exist. We can therefore assume that it goes back even further than that. Indeed, the founding myth of classicism (the revived interest in classical antiquity from the fourteenth century onward) is the execution of Socrates for "corrupting the youth" and "blasphemy," detailed in Jacob Mchangama's excellent *Free Speech: A History from Socrates to Social Media.*[19] Indeed, blasphemy is one of the oldest alleged justifications for censorship, right alongside lèse-majesté (insulting the ruler), treason, sedition, and libel.

While the ancient Greeks made a lot of arguments in favor of their recognized forms of free speech, it shouldn't come as a great surprise that freedom of speech wasn't as discussed and valued between the time of the fall of the democratic city-states and the advent of the printing press. After all, if you can't reach most people by any means, arguments for freedom of speech have very little practical meaning. But as soon as widespread dissemination of ideas was possible, advocates for "freedom of the press" cropped up everywhere.

"John Stuart Mill's central arguments in On Liberty remain undefeated, including one of his strongest arguments in favor of freedom of speech—Mill's trident—of which I have never heard a persuasive refutation."

Truly robust protection for freedom of speech was a long time in the making and stood in stark contrast with older forces of conformity, conservatism, dogmatism, and religiosity. In other words, freedom of speech has mostly been the exception throughout history, and has only become both legally and culturally powerful, even in the United States, in the last century. Though the First Amendment was passed in 1791, it was not until 1925 that its freedom of speech guarantee was interpreted as having real meaning for the United States,[20] and it was not until the 1960s that this freedom was consistently protected.

One thing that can be very frustrating to First Amendment defenders is how often we hear age-old arguments about free speech and censorship being brought up as if they are new or innovative. Among the most frustrating is the assertion that speech is indistinguishable from violence because it either causes stress or psychological harm (see Argument #1). This is a very old idea, and is arguably the moral intuition undergirding cultures that emphasize the preservation of honor, and prescribe that slights against one's honor should be dealt with by duels or honor-killings. Indeed, nineteenth-century slave owners, including John C. Calhoun, even argued that abolitionists' arguments were offensive to their dignity.[21]

While the arguments for censorship are almost all extremely old, many of the arguments for freedom of speech are new and constantly evolving. Despite his oft-misrepresented footnote mention of "the paradox of tolerance,"[22] Karl Popper was an innovative thinker about freedom of speech, as was Lenny Bruce, and as are Jonathan Rauch, Jonathan Haidt, and the many people synthesizing free-speech arguments with law, history, and the latest psychological and sociological research. Another compelling new argument in favor of free speech is how the establishment of norms of dissent in cockpits and operating rooms have led to dramatic improvements in the safety of both airline traffic and surgery.[23]

John Stuart Mill's central arguments in *On Liberty* remain undefeated, including one of his strongest arguments in favor of freedom of speech—Mill's trident—of which I have never heard a persuasive refutation.[24]

Mill's trident holds that, for any given belief, there are three options:

1. You are wrong; in which case freedom of speech is essential to allow people to correct you.
2. You are partially correct; in which case you need freedom of speech and contrary viewpoints to help you attain a more precise understanding of what the truth really is.

3. You are 100 percent correct. In this unlikely event, you still need people to argue with you, to try to contradict you, and to try to prove you wrong. Why? Because if you never have to defend your points of view, there is a very good chance you don't really understand them, and that you hold them the same way you would hold a prejudice or superstition. It's only through arguing with contrary viewpoints that you come to understand why what you believe is true, and are able to explain your position to others more persuasively.

Mill's trident remains true in the age of the internet. Meta's move away from centralized fact-checking and to a system of Community Notes is possible in part because of the strength of Mill's trident. Media critics wanted to portray the ending of social media censorship as the Facebook parent company's capitulating to political populism.[25] But it was less a capitulation to a party and more a reckoning with reality.

The problem with viewing a move away from fact-checkers as a net negative is that fact-checking didn't work the way we all wanted it to work. Fact checkers are sometimes wrong,[26] and even when they get it right,[27] the existence of top-down content filtering reduces trust and confidence in all content on a platform. As David Moschella of the Information Technology and Innovation Forum explained, "it's not that these groups [government, media, scientists, and fact-checkers] can't be trusted; it's that they all have their own agendas and can't be trusted to be right all of the time."[28]

Fact-checkers have *reduced* trust in platforms. In FIRE's social media report released in 2024, we found that "61 percent of Democrats, 62 percent of independents, and 73 percent of Republicans don't trust social media companies to be fair about what can be posted on their platform."[29]

As I observed on X, this was entirely predictable, given that fact-checkers, both on and off campus, have rightfully lost the public's trust.[30] Viewing a retreat from a system that doesn't work (and undermines epistemic trust) as a concession to Trump is short-sighted and self-defeating.

Are community notes perfect? No. But saying a crowd-sourced system is imperfect doesn't mean it isn't the best system we have available. And its greatest virtue is that it does not anoint anyone to sit as the "arbiter of truth." All of it rests on Mill's trident and the arguments that make free speech work.

Argument #6: Free Speech Is Right-wing

Free Speech is nothing but a conservative talking point.

Nadine Strossen:

It is true that too many conservatives are eager to support free speech when conservative speakers or views are the targets of censorship—and less eager to support free speech in other circumstances. However, the same is also true for too many liberals and progressives. Multiple commentators have quipped that most people believe in "free speech for *me* (or people who agree with me), but not for *thee*."[1]

Principled supporters of free speech should neutrally support freedom "even for the thought that [they] hate," to quote former Supreme Court Justice Oliver Wendell Holmes.[2] Such an even-handed approach lends more credibility and influence to their advocacy, which can't then be dismissed as mere result-oriented lip service to free speech values only when the speech at issue accords with their own political, cultural, or other values.

For example, FIRE's consistent advocacy of free speech rights on campus, for students and faculty members all across the ideological spectrum, has earned it well-deserved respect as a principled free speech champion, lending weight to its arguments in all cases. The same has been true of the ACLU, which has controversially defended free speech even for racist speakers whose views are antithetical to the ACLU's own championship of racial justice. While many critics object to such work, many supporters of it—including leading African American civil rights champions—are convinced that the ACLU's racial justice advocacy is strengthened by its support for robust free speech rights, extending even to opponents of racial justice.

One prominent example is Eleanor Holmes Norton, the longtime District of Columbia Representative in Congress. Norton began her distinguished career as an ACLU staff lawyer in the 1960s, when she (successfully) defended freedom of speech for a number of white supremacists, including Alabama's notorious arch-segregationist Governor George Wallace and an Ohio Ku Klux Klan leader, Clarence Brandenburg. In a 2019 interview, discussing her work on those cases, Norton said:

> I relished those cases, because I knew that the left and civil rights activists were the primary users of free speech, so the racist cases made our principled arguments even stronger. My friends at SNCC, the Student Nonviolent Coordinating Committee, were not always convinced by this approach because "what's sauce for the goose would not have the same flavor for the gander." But I knew we were winning all those cases because we were winning for both sides.[3]

Examples abound of free speech principles that are forged in cases where the immediate beneficiary espouses a particular controversial ideology, which are then deployed to the benefit of speakers and audience members with diametrically different ideologies. In particular, there are many examples where the immediate beneficiaries of speech-protective

Supreme Court rulings are conservative organizations, individuals, and ideas, yet quite quickly these rulings also redound to the benefit of their progressive counterparts. I will cite just two recent examples: the Supreme Court's 2023 decision in *303 Creative v. Elenis*,[4] and its 2024 decision in *National Rifle Association v. Vullo*.[5]

303 Creative sustained a First Amendment challenge to a Colorado law barring discrimination on the basis of sexual orientation, as enforced against a website designer, Lorie Smith, who challenged Colorado's effort to force her to create websites purveying views that violated her own, including websites for same-sex weddings. That decision has been a mainstay of arguments being made in 2025 on behalf of universities, arguing that the First Amendment bars the Trump Administration from enforcing federal laws against antisemitic discrimination by forcing the universities to (among other things) restrict and punish certain campus expression.

Likewise, the universities and other institutions—including law firms—that the Trump Administration has subjected to various punitive measures have invoked the *NRA* ruling, which upheld the NRA's claim that government officials may not punish individuals or organizations based on disapproval of their viewpoints. In the *NRA* case itself, a Democratic New York State official had sought to punish the NRA for its positions on gun regulation issues, which that official disfavored. Correspondingly, the Trump Administration is seeking to punish universities, law firms, and others for their positions that President Trump disfavors, on issues including DEI, the war in the Middle East, and presidential elections.

In deciding to represent the NRA—despite strong criticism, including even from some of its state-based affiliates[6]—the ACLU specifically predicted that, if the

Supreme Court did not invalidate the New York official's action, a second Trump administration would pursue similar actions against its ideological opponents, including the ACLU itself (which had brought many complaints against actions by the first Trump administration that, as courts ruled, violated fundamental constitutional rights). In March 2024, before the Supreme Court had ruled on the case, the ACLU's Executive Director, Anthony Romero, responded to critics of the ACLU's NRA representation with a powerful, prophetic statement:

> We are deeply concerned that if regulators can threaten the NRA for their political views in New York state, they can come after the ACLU and allied organizations in places where our agendas are unpopular. . . . In a second Trump administration . . . political leaders . . . may seek to go after their rivals the way New York targeted the NRA. The principal issue at stake in this case is . . . preventing government blacklists of advocacy groups. Indeed, the timing couldn't be better for drawing a bright line that would help bind a future Trump administration and other government officials who misuse their power.[7]

Many free speech skeptics from the left end of the political spectrum opposed the free speech arguments that were made by and on behalf of Lorie Smith and the NRA—because these skeptics disfavored their messages. One hopes that these critics have reconsidered their opposition in light of how essential the resulting free speech rulings now are in resisting the Trump Administration's efforts to suppress speakers and messages it disfavors.

> "Consistent defense of free speech for all speakers and views is not only the principled approach; it is also the strategically sound one."

After the Supreme Court issued its *303 Creative* decision, I coauthored an op-ed with Kristen Waggoner, the Executive Director of the Alliance Defending Freedom (ADF), a conservative religious rights organization, which had represented Smith. We explained why—despite our significant disagreements about other important issues—we concurred in endorsing the Supreme Court's ruling in this case, explaining that it followed from many precedents that had protected speakers with a wide range of views, and predicting that it would benefit advocates on all sides of all issues. Here's a small excerpt:

> The court ruled the government may not compel Smith to endorse same-sex marriage. But it did so because of fundamental free speech tenets that benefit all of us, regardless of our views on same-sex marriage or any other issue. . . . If we don't protect the speech we loathe, we can't protect the speech we love. . . . Following a long line of cases, [this decision] rejects government efforts to coerce ideological conformity.[8]

So, yes, when conservative speakers and perspectives are censored, some conservatives may opportunistically invoke free speech principles specifically because they support the particular content of the speech at issue. Yet it behooves liberals, progressives, and other non-conservatives also to invoke free speech principles in these situations, because that is the most effective way to ensure freedom of speech for those whose ideas they support. In other words, consistent defense of free speech for all speakers and views is not only the principled approach; it is also the strategically sound one.[9]

Greg Lukianoff:

Free speech is neither a conservative nor liberal idea. It is an eternally radical idea.[10]

In our hopelessly polarized society, too many people begin by asking, "*So, is free speech a conservative or progressive idea? Is it right-wing or left-wing?*" If the answer is *left-wing*, throngs on the right assume it can be ignored. If the answer is *right-wing*, many on the left feel absolved from having to take it seriously. At various points—even in recent history—both major political parties in the United States have claimed to represent free speech at the same time as both have been extremely hostile to free speech.[11]

True support for free expression—especially extreme political speech with which you disagree—is a rare and, indeed, historically radical idea. This point is so important that I even named my blog The Eternally Radical Idea.[12]

Refusing to engage with an idea by rejecting it as "right-wing" is very similar to the outermost barricade of what my co-author Rikki Schlott and I identified as the Perfect Rhetorical Fortress (defending the left) in our book, *The Canceling of the American Mind.*[13] (The right has its own analog with a similar first layer.)[14] In this layer, an idea is rejected with an ideological ad-hominem levied against its evangelist. I have since come to call this "fashcasting," a contraction recommended by Kat Rosenfield[15]; the tactic of dismissing an idea by calling the people who espouse it "conservative," "right-wing," "far right," "fascist," or, lately, "neo-confederate," whether they actually are these things or not.[16]

In fact, fashcasting is most often used against people who *don't* self-identify as conservative. If you can argue that someone is "right-adjacent," even if they consider themselves liberal or progressive—and even if they've voted Democrat their entire lives—they can be dismissed as well. As we point out in *Canceling*, essentially any liberal critic of cancel culture or the excesses of what Tim Urban calls social justice fundamentalism can suddenly fall under the "conservative" label: Jon Ronson, Jonathan Chait, Alice Dreger, Meghan Daum, Noam Chomsky, Gloria Steinem, Salman Rushdie (the last three of whom signed the Harper's Letter[17]), and yours truly, just to name a few.

Argument #7: About That Crowded Theater and the Marketplace of Ideas

The Supreme Court was right when it said that you can't shout "Fire!" in a crowded theater but wrong when it said that the marketplace of ideas will lead to truth.

Nadine Strossen:

Actually, both of these constantly-invoked purported paraphrases of famous Supreme Court opinions by Justice Oliver Wendell Holmes are *distorted* versions of what Holmes actually said.

What he actually said continues to ring true as sensible bases for punishing and protecting speech, respectively.

First, what Holmes actually said about shouting "*fire!*" is consistent with the basic precept that speech may not be punished solely based on the disfavored or generally feared nature of its message, but rather only when, considered in its overall context, it directly causes or imminently threatens certain specific serious harm. Only if someone "falsely" shouts *Fire!* in a theater, when in fact there is no fire, will the expression be considered as punishable.

Second, what Holmes actually said about the marketplace of ideas is that the free exchange of ideas is *more likely* to lead to truth than is any kind of centralized, censorial control.

Here are the actual Holmes statements, with some surrounding context:

Schenck v United States, 249 U.S. 47, 52 (1919) (Holmes, writing for a unanimous court):

> The character of every act depends upon the circumstances in which it is done. . . . **The most stringent protection of free speech would not protect a man falsely shouting fire in a theatre and causing a panic**. . . . The question in every case is whether the words used are used in such circumstances and are of such a nature as to create a clear and present danger that they will bring about the substantive evils that Congress has a right to prevent (emphasis added).

Abrams v United States, 250 U.S. 616, 630 (1919) (Holmes, dissenting, joined by Brandeis):

> Persecution for the expression of opinions seems to me perfectly logical. If you have no doubt of your premises or your power, and want a certain result with all your heart, you naturally express your wishes in law, and sweep away all opposition. To allow opposition by speech seems to indicate that you think the speech impotent . . . or that you do not care wholeheartedly for the result, or that you doubt either your power or your premises. **But when men have realized that time has upset many fighting faiths, they may come to believe even more than they believe the very foundations of their own conduct that the ultimate good desired is better reached by free trade in ideas —that the best test of truth is the power of the thought to get itself**

> **accepted in the competition of the market, and that truth is the only ground upon which their wishes safely can be carried out. That, at any rate, is the theory of our Constitution. It is an experiment, as all life is an experiment** (emphasis added).

Holmes's argument in *Abrams* was far from an outright prediction that free speech would inevitably lead to truth. Rather, he explained, "the theory of our Constitution" is that free speech is "better" suited for truth-seeking than censorship, but he acknowledged that this approach "is an experiment, as all life is an experiment," as it is necessarily "based upon imperfect knowledge." Nonetheless, he went on to conclude that "while that experiment is part of our system . . . we should be eternally vigilant against attempts to check the expression of opinions that we loathe and believe to be fraught with death, unless they so imminently threaten immediate interference with the lawful and pressing purposes of the law that an immediate check is required to save the country." In short, a rigorous search for truth demands that all ideas must be subject to debate and discussion through robust free speech—including that very concept itself.

Evidence accumulated through our ongoing First Amendment "experiment" continues to reaffirm that free speech is a less imperfect vehicle for pursuing truth than is the censorial alternative. For example, it is now an accepted theory that COVID originated from a leak in a laboratory in Wuhan, China.[1] Government officials, experts, and reporters had condemned this explanation as a conspiracy theory[2] (or even attributed it to racism)[3] after the pandemic's outbreak in early 2020, and it had been suppressed in major traditional[4] and social media outlets.[5] Likewise, prominent scientists who advocated at least investigating this theory were pilloried and even subjected to retaliatory measures.[6] Yet, in the spring of 2021 the theory was rehabilitated as at least warranting serious consideration.[7] And in January 2025, the CIA released an analysis that started under the Biden administration and found no smoking gun, but that the lab leak theory was more probable than the natural-origin theory.[8]

Despite the initial exclusion of the lab leak theory from key segments of the marketplace of ideas, that overall marketplace was still functioning. Had that not been the case, we would have been denied critically important ongoing investigations and discussions, with their potentially enormous impact on public health and national security.

> "A rigorous search for truth demands that all ideas must be subject to debate and discussion through robust free speech—including that very concept itself."

In 1984, Professor Melville Nimmer well captured the core skeptical, relativistic notion underlying the truth-seeking rationale for free speech. Quoting Holmes's marketplace metaphor, he asked, "if acceptance of an idea in the competition of the market is not the 'best test'" of its truth, what "is the alternative?" Logically, as he concluded, the answer could "only be acceptance of an idea by some individual or group narrower than that of the public at large."[9] Are "We the People," who wield sovereign power in our democratic republic, willing to entrust any individual or subgroup with the incalculable power of determining which ideas are fit for our consumption and discussion?

Are we willing to entrust that power to any government official or body?

In addition to the persuasive truth-seeking rationale for strongly protecting free speech, there are multiple other important rationales, each of which provides an independent justification for such protection. Important additional rationales for protecting free speech include its essential roles in: democratic self-governance; facilitating individual autonomy and self-expression; serving as an escape valve for conflicts, furthering their peaceful resolution; promoting tolerance; promoting all other human rights; and Greg's compelling "pure informational theory" (discussed immediately below). One indication of the force of these pro-free speech rationales is the fact that freedom of speech has been strongly protected not only in the US Constitution, but also in its counterparts in countries around the world, as well as in major international and regional human rights treaties.

Greg Lukianoff:

Anyone who says "you can't shout *Fire!* in a crowded theater" is showing that they don't know much about the principles of free speech, or free speech law—or history.

This old canard, a favorite reference of censorship apologists, needs to be retired. It's repeatedly and inappropriately used to justify speech limitations. People have been using this cliché as if it had some legal meaning, while First Amendment lawyers roll their eyes and point out that it is, in fact, as Alan Dershowitz puts it, "a caricature of logical argumentation."[10]

The phrase is a misquotation of an analogy made in a 1919 Supreme Court opinion that upheld the imprisonment of three people—a newspaper editor, a pamphlet publisher, and a public speaker—who argued that military conscription was wrong. The Court said that anti-war speech in wartime is like "falsely shouting fire in a theater and causing a panic," and it justified the ban with a dubious analogy to the longstanding principle that the First Amendment doesn't protect speech that incites people to physical violence. But the Supreme Court abandoned the logic of that case more than fifty years ago. That this trope originated as a purported justification for what has long since been deemed unconstitutional censorship underscores its illegitimacy as an asserted standard for assessing speech limitations. And yet, the crowded-theater cliché endures, as if it were some venerable legal principle.

Oh, and notice that the Court's objection was only to "*falsely* shouting *fire!*" If there is, in fact, a fire in a crowded theater, please let everyone know.

As for the "marketplace of ideas," this metaphor is vivid, relatable, memorable . . . and incomplete. The marketplace of ideas metaphor makes a lot of sense in the political arena, where one group seeks to prevail over another. It perhaps makes even more sense in the world of academic scholarship, where scholars battle it out to determine whose version of the world, from physics to ancient history, will prevail. But beyond that, the "marketplace" metaphor doesn't really capture free speech's most fundamental function: *Freedom of speech gives you a fighting chance to know the world as it really is*. I call that the "pure informational theory" of freedom of speech.

Under the "marketplace of ideas" theory, someone's expression of an inaccurate belief could be seen as having zero or even negative value. Under the pure informational theory, however, knowing that the inaccurate opinion exists has tremendous value, especially if it is widely held. While the marketplace of ideas metaphor does a good job of explaining that we must tolerate beliefs that are later proved to be false—because as a practical matter it often takes a great deal of time to learn that a belief is false, and sometimes you never know—it doesn't expressly acknowledge the existence of a misconception as an important fact in and of itself.

This limitation of the marketplace metaphor has been used by some scholars and academics to dismiss or diminish the value of free expression.[11] Their argument goes one of two ways.

According to one argument, freedom of speech is justified on the basis of establishing "truth," but since we now "know" that objective truth is either impossible or nearly impossible to establish, all we are left with are competing stories with equivalent inherent worth, and all that matters is a political victory of one side's "story" over the other. Not coincidentally, the advocates of this argument often seem to think that it is *their* ideology that should fill the gap, not taking sufficiently seriously that anyone else's ideology could just as easily do so. In such a system, the winning ideology will belong to whoever has the most power; and the critics of truth will come to discover that truth was all that stood between them and the imposed will of the powerful.

The second argument typically points to the apparent inability of the good ideas to ever finally defeat and drive from the earth bad ideas. Some bad ideas shamble around like zombies decades or centuries after their supposed "defeat" in the marketplace of ideas. For example, it's been known that the earth is (roughly) spherical since at least Aristotle (and, arguably, Pythagoras more than a century earlier). Nevertheless, belief in a flat earth has seemingly resurged with the rise of the internet, with a number of celebrity adherents (who presumably can afford to find the truth for themselves, but inexplicably have not).[12]

The unknowability of objective truth and the seeming

immortality of bad ideas pose problems for the marketplace model, but they hold far less relevance for a pure informational theory of freedom of speech. Under that theory, the goal of freedom of speech is not limited to establishing the objective "big-T Truth" about, say, the Platonic form of beauty, goodness, or squareness, but rather, the more mundane "little-T truth" of expressed opinion, preference, or belief. Knowing that individuals believe in conspiracy theories about lizard people is valuable, not because it might be true (call me unscientific, but I'm willing to call this one as obviously false), but because you might want to know that someone believes in lizard people before dating them or making them your primary care physician. On a larger scale (no pun intended), it's useful to know whether paranoid delusions are common within a population.

If finding objective truth were the only value of freedom of expression, there would be little value to studying history. Most of human thought in history has been mistaken in its assumptions and beliefs about the world and each other; nevertheless, understanding things like superstitions, folk medicine, and apocryphal family histories has significance and value. Many disciplines recognize this intrinsically; few Greek historians say they got into the field so they could determine what it was *really like* to hang out with Zeus. Instead, we want to know everything about ourselves and our histories, even when it reveals that our collective beliefs have been, in hindsight, manifestly false. The marketplace metaphor does not capture these crucial aspects of free speech.

A fitting metaphor for the pure informational theory of free speech might be "the lab in the looking glass." Imagine being a scientist and showing up to a new fully staffed laboratory with all of the best equipment that's ever been invented. You have not been told about the project you will be working on, but there is a huge curtain in front of you. The director of the project announces that the study is the most challenging that has ever been undertaken and you will not be able to finish it in your lifetime, but even knowing a little bit more about the subject will be of nearly limitless value. He pulls back the curtain to reveal a gigantic mirror looking right back at you.

You and your colleagues are to be the subjects. The project: to know everything about you and everything related to you. Where you come from, as recently as this morning and as far back as the Big Bang and maybe before; what makes you tick; what your societies look like; what attracts or repels you; what makes you angry or sad or ambivalent; how much you would pay for a bottle of wine from Napa; how much your neighbor would be willing to pay to be more beautiful; what kind of planet you live on; what kind of stellar objects you can see; what the smallest unit of matter is that makes up you and your world. This is the Project of Human Knowledge. It is basically the project that humanism began many centuries ago: to know as much about us and our world as we can.

Once we take off our "marketplace of ideas" glasses and start to look through the lens of the pure informational theory of freedom of speech, the answers to many free speech questions suddenly become quite obvious.

> "Both for scientific reasons and for our success as a democratic republic, we need to know more, not less about the ideas in our fellow humans' heads. . . . It is always important to know what people really believe, especially when the belief is perplexing or troubling."

For example, let's say you were studying the prairie vole, a small rodent that lives in Australia and North America and is famously monogamous. You then discover one prairie vole that is a regular Don Draper, mating with any vole it can find. Do you then say, "Well, this is an aberration from commonly accepted prairie vole norms, so I must not report it?" Or maybe, "This prairie vole violates my personal sense of morality, and therefore I shall ignore it!" Of course not. You ask yourself, "I wonder why this prairie vole is different? I bet we could learn a lot by looking into it." And, indeed, research into prairie voles is producing extraordinarily interesting findings about genetic and hormonal influences on monogamy and polygyny.

The same is true for the human animal. Both for scientific reasons and for our success as a democratic republic, we need to know more, not less about the ideas in our fellow humans' heads. I call it my "Iron Law": it is always important to know what people really believe, especially when the belief is perplexing or troubling. Conversely, in the overwhelming majority of scenarios, you are not safer or better off for knowing less about what people really think.

The "lab in the looking glass" metaphor can also explain a whole lot more about the First Amendment than the Darwinian marketplace of ideas. Again, the marketplace of ideas has some explanatory power relating to political speech and academic freedom, but it does a poor job of explaining why, for example, sexual expression should be protected. Erotic, violent, or otherwise provocative art has to be awkwardly transformed into an argument that could "win" in order to have a place within the marketplace of ideas. However, taking the looking glass laboratory approach, erotic or violent art must be allowed because it both reflects the deepest human urges and tells us more about human nature.

The lab in the looking glass theory even better explains the major flaw in thinking about hate speech. Yes, the expression of hate can cause real emotional pain, and that is why some constitutional lawyers argue that it is "low value" speech. However, if you view hate speech from the purely informational standpoint, it is of course absolutely crucial to know if someone is a bigot for a vast number of reasons when, for example, deciding to go into business with them; electing them to public office; putting them in charge of your human resources department; hiring them to supervise your children; or, more generally, in knowing about the tensions in your community, county, state, or country. Or as I wrote years ago, in my first attempt to present this theory: "Forcing hate speech underground by banning it is like taking Xanax for syphilis. You may briefly feel better about your horrible disease, but your sickness will only get worse."

There's still so much we don't yet know about the natural world we inhabit, and about biology, human nature, and group psychology. We will answer these questions and many more if we are willing to enter the looking-glass lab and see ourselves as we really are. To do that requires a kind of radical openness rooted in an expanded understanding of the societal role of freedom of speech.

Argument #8: Free Speech Protects Power

Free speech is the tool of the powerful, not the powerless.

Nadine Strossen:

People who have access to resources that facilitate communication—not only money, but at least as importantly education and technology—can more meaningfully exercise their freedom of speech to communicate more effectively with a larger audience. That fact, however, does not logically support the conclusion that freedom of speech should be curtailed. Rather, it supports the conclusion that our society must continue to vigorously promote everyone's full and equal access to the means for effective communication.

In 1960, journalist A. J. Liebling famously quipped that "freedom of the press is guaranteed only to those who own one."[1] Advocates of both free speech and equal rights have been working to change that impoverished free speech reality, including by leading the fight for a free and open internet, which can potentially make everyone the functional equivalent of a printing press owner. The internet and mobile phones have empowered grassroots groups to mobilize for multiple causes—including Black Lives Matter and Me Too—that could not have gained such traction through the vastly more expensive, exclusionary communications tools of earlier eras.

"It is precisely those who lack political or economic power who are the most dependent on robust freedom of speech."

It is sad but true that not only freedom of speech, but also other rights, are too often more fully enjoyed by those with more resources. The solution to this problem is hardly to reduce the scope of the rights, but rather, to increase the ability of more people to meaningfully exercise them. Consider, for example, the fundamental right to life itself.

In the US, people charged with capital crimes are far more likely to be sentenced to death, and actually executed, if they are indigent and hence dependent on overburdened and under-resourced public defenders. The answer to this problem is hardly to reduce constitutional protections against capital punishment, but rather, to increase the resources that permit poorer people to benefit from those constitutional protections.

There is another fatal flaw in the argument that freedom of speech further entrenches the privilege and power of those who already have both: It is precisely those who lack political or economic power who are the most dependent on robust freedom of speech.

Throughout US history (and in other countries), equal rights and social justice movements have gained momentum through forceful exercise of free speech rights to advocate and demonstrate, litigate and lobby. Conversely, censorship is consistently wielded in an effort to stymie these causes. In short, it is the disempowered, not the powerful, who have the most to gain from strong free speech protection, and the most to lose from its weakening. To this day, state and local governments around the US have been disproportionately enforcing existing laws, and enacting new ones, to stifle protesters for progressive causes including racial justice, police reform, and environmental activism.

Greg Lukianoff:

The powerful do well under virtually any system of government. They're not the ones who need freedom of speech. Its purpose is precisely to protect minority opinions and those who are unpopular with powerful people.

For most of history, the rich and powerful were protected by their wealth and power. Then, when democracies first emerged, the majority set the laws, and, because of that, their majority positions were protected by law. You only need a separate concept of freedom of speech or a law like the First Amendment to protect people, ideas, and arguments that are not already otherwise protected by the right to vote or some other power.

The ones who enforce the rules are, by definition, powerful. In a country with strong protections for freedom of speech, the powerful are barred from using the legal system to attack the powerless for their speech. If you empower the government to censor, you are giving the powerful more power.

"If you eliminate or restrain freedom of speech, the powerful are just as powerful, with the added benefit of pre-silenced critics."

Think of it this way: All civil rights and liberties, including free speech, are properly understood as *limitations* on the power of government. And in the United States, those rights are meant to accrue evenly across the population, regardless of economic status, race, or any other factor. Any inequity in the application of those rights is a limitation of the political, social, and other forces around those rights, not a glitch in the rights themselves. Free speech is a tool to call out those systems and correct them. And if you eliminate or restrain freedom of speech, the powerful are just as powerful, with the added benefit of pre-silenced critics. A good intellectual exercise before passing a new law is to consider how your worst enemy would use that law—and thinking about that is even more important when imagining restrictions on free speech.

The idea that we can trust the government to use the power to restrain speech in a way that defends the powerless is not borne out by history. If you want to give whoever is powerful censorship tools to protect the marginalized, do you trust that they will use it well? Look back at Argument #3, about hate speech. Under all of those laws, governments were given the power to censor for the purpose of promoting tolerance. How is that working out?

We have seen dramatic swings in our executive branch across the last three administrations; how comfortable are you that the power you gave to one would be wielded in a way you like by the other?

Argument #9: Misinformation and Disinformation Aren't Free Speech

Free speech's core purpose is to promote democracy, but mis- and disinformation undermine democracy.

Nadine Strossen:

Efforts to censor speech labeled as misinformation or disinformation inherently endanger dissent, criticism of the government, and civil rights movements—thus undermining liberty, equality, and democracy alike.

Consistent with the emergency principle, the government may punish false speech when it directly, immediately causes specific serious harm. Important examples of punishable false speech include defamation, fraud, and perjury. The terms "disinformation" and "misinformation" have no specific legal meaning, but they are widely used to describe false or misleading speech that cannot constitutionally be punished precisely because their potential harms are speculative.

Current debates show that one person's cherished truth is someone else's despised or feared "fake news." Speech that critics seek to suppress as disinformation almost never consists of objectively verifiable/falsifiable facts alone, but rather also involves subjective matters of interpretation and analysis. After all, speakers who intentionally or recklessly utter false factual statements often may be constitutionally punished under existing laws such as those against fraud and defamation. In contrast, though, the Supreme Court has ruled that "under the First Amendment there is no such thing as a false idea. However pernicious an opinion may seem, we depend for its correction . . . on the competition of other ideas."[1]

> "Given the inescapable elasticity of the concept of disinformation, restrictions on it can easily be wielded against important information, even in democratic countries."

If government were permitted to determine which ideas should be punishable as "false," most vulnerable would be ideas that challenge government policy. Until the Supreme Court's historic 1964 *New York Times v. Sullivan* decision,[2] which reined in the concept of punishable defamation, Southern officials systematically pursued multiple defamation lawsuits against civil rights activists and national media outlets that reported on their advocacy for even trivial factual inaccuracies, with the specific goal of stifling both sets of speakers. In short, the pre-1964 defamation law, which permitted the government to punish disinformation, was weaponized against the government's critics.[3]

To this day, expression by racial justice advocates continues to be assailed as disinformation (as well as hate speech and extremist or terrorist speech).[4] For instance, an NPR story quoted Mike Gonzalez, a senior fellow with the Heritage Foundation, as stating: "I feel that Black Lives Matter is one of the greatest sources of disinformation . . . They have manipulated the good nature of many people."[5]

To be sure, such charges of disinformation themselves constitute protected speech—indeed, the very type of "counterspeech" that is the appropriate response to any speech that is believed to be false or misleading. My point is that government should not be empowered to deploy this malleable concept as the basis for censorship.

The inherent problems with censoring disinformation in general plague recent laws that were touted as restricting COVID-related disinformation in particular. *The Economist* reported in 2021 that "censorious governments are abusing fake news laws," invoking the pandemic as "an excuse to gag reporters" and to silence critics of their anti-pandemic policies.[6] Given the inescapable elasticity of the concept of disinformation, restrictions on it can easily be wielded against important information, even in democratic countries. Throughout the pandemic, we witnessed constantly evolving and shifting views among expert individuals and agencies, as they steadily gathered and analyzed additional data. Yesterday's life-endangering disinformation can—and has—become today's life-protecting gospel. As one example, recall the CDC's (Center for Disease Control and Prevention's) changing edicts about mask-wearing.[7]

Because of these unavoidable problems with outlawing COVID-related disinformation, in 2020, the ACLU brought a lawsuit against Puerto Rico's laws on point.[8] The complainants were two prominent investigative journalists, who explained that "developing stories on matters of immense public concern are often complex, contentious, and murky," so that "inadvertent inaccuracies are inevitable even in the most thoroughly vetted reporting."[9] Shortly after the laws went into effect, the Puerto Rican government charged a leading clergyman with allegedly disseminating false information on WhatsApp, about a rumored executive order to close all businesses.[10] However, only a short time later, the Governor did issue just such an order.[11]

In 2023, the judge in the ACLU case struck down Puerto Rico's law, declaring that "the watchdog function of speech is never more vital than during a large-scale crisis."[12] Touting the time-honored counterspeech approach, the judge observed: "Instead of criminalizing speech, the Legislature could simply have required the Government to use its multiple communications platforms to present a complete and accurate description of the facts" about COVID and other emergencies.[13]

The judge's recommended strategy is supported by multiple studies, which have concluded that the most fruitful anti-disinformation tool is accurate information that can check its spread and influence, including: proactive dissemination of accurate information; targeted responses to specific disinformation; and preemptive general educational approaches, enhancing information literacy and critical media skills. Psychological research shows that even more effective than debunking disinformation after its distribution is "pre-bunking," or showing people how misinformation is created and spread before they encounter it.[14] As authors of one 2020 study explained: "Pre-emptively warning and exposing people to weakened doses of misinformation can cultivate 'mental antibodies' against fake news."[15] In sum, in contrast with censorship, these "counterspeech"/"more speech" strategies not only are more compatible with free speech and democracy; they also are more effective in promoting truth.

Greg Lukianoff:

"Misinformation" is another word for falsehoods that are spread unintentionally. This is distinct from "disinformation," which is the word for falsehoods that are intentionally spread—otherwise known as lies.

Contrary to how proponents of granting First Amendment exceptions for "misinformation" and "disinformation" like to frame it, these are not easily discernible or definable categories. Rather, they are an exception that swallows the rule of free speech. They allow for virtual omnipotence on the part of government officials to determine what is and is not true—and therefore what you and I are allowed to see, read, and hear. This grants them immense power, which they will of course abuse to suit their own purposes and biases.

We aren't great at knowing what's true to begin with. The COVID-related reversals on masking are one example, but there are many more in medicine alone. Thousands of years of bloodletting until the mid-nineteenth century,[16] menthol cigarettes offered to ease colds in the 1940s,[17] homosexuality identified as a mental disorder until the 1970s,[18] the belief that stress is the primary cause of ulcers until the 1980s[19]—we thought we knew what was true, and looking back, it's very clear we did not.

The biggest realization of the Enlightenment (which is better thought of as the discovery of our ignorance) is that the truth is extremely hard to know. It takes an arduous and never-ending process to even attempt to do so, and we often fail. Jonathan Rauch has identified two rules for the search for truth:

> **The fallibilist rule:** *No one gets the final say*. You may claim that a statement is established as knowledge only if it can be debunked, in principle, and only insofar as it withstands attempts to debunk it. That is, you are entitled to claim that a statement is objectively true only insofar as it is both checkable and has stood up to checking, and not otherwise.

> **The empirical rule:** *No one has personal authority.* You may claim that a statement has been established as knowledge only insofar as the method used to check it gives the same result regardless of the identity of the checker, and regardless of the source of the statement.[20]

That this process takes time is why the government is not in a position to dictate truth; it's in a position to create the environment where truth can eventually be found. This is why the "Spirit of Liberty" that Learned Hand described in his famous 1944 speech is "not too sure that it is right" and "seeks to understand the mind of other men and women."[21] We give people the freedom to find and speak truth, which requires the freedom to be wrong about it, too.

Government officials may want omnipotence, but even if they had it, they would still not be omniscient. And that makes any omnipotence they might gain dangerous.

Argument #10: About the Holocaust and the Rwandan Genocide

The rise of Hitler and Nazism in Germany and the Rwandan genocide epitomize why we should censor hateful and extremist speech.

Nadine Strossen:

Given the horrors of the Holocaust, even diehard free speech stalwarts would support stricter hate speech laws if they would have averted that atrocity. That is certainly the case for me, as the daughter of a German-born Holocaust survivor, who nearly died at Buchenwald. That also is true for the prominent international human rights champion Aryeh Neier, who managed to flee from Nazi Germany with his immediate family when he was a child, while the Nazis slaughtered his extended family.

Neier was the ACLU's executive director in 1977–78, when the ACLU successfully defended the First Amendment rights of neo-Nazis to demonstrate in Skokie, Illinois, a town that had a large Jewish population, many of whom were Holocaust survivors. Because Neier is a justly renowned free speech proponent, many readers will be surprised to learn of his statement that he would have supported censoring the Nazis if that would have forestalled their ascension to power:

> I am unwilling to put anything, even love of free speech, ahead of detestation of the Nazis. . . . I could not bring myself to advocate freedom of speech in Skokie if I did not believe that the chances are best for preventing a repetition of the Holocaust in a society where every incursion on freedom is resisted. Freedom has its risks. Suppression of freedom, I believe, is a sure prescription for disaster.[1]

Proponents of additional restrictions on hate speech—beyond the context-based limits that the First Amendment permits, such as when the speech constitutes a targeted threat or harassment—assume that such restrictions might have prevented the spread of Nazi ideology in Germany. But the historical record belies this assumption.

"The major problem with Germany's response to rising Nazism was not that the Nazis enjoyed too much free speech, but that the Nazis literally got away with murder. In effect, they stole free speech from everyone else, including anti-Nazis, Jews, and other minorities."

Throughout the Nazis' rise to power, there were laws on the books criminalizing hateful, discriminatory speech, which were similar to contemporary hate speech laws in Germany and elsewhere. As noted by Alan Borovoy, general counsel of the Canadian Civil Liberties Association, when he set out his/the CCLA's opposition to Canada's current hate speech legislation:

> Remarkably, pre-Hitler Germany had laws very much like the Canadian anti-hate law. Moreover, those laws were enforced with some vigour. During the fifteen years before Hitler came to power, there were more than two hundred prosecutions based on anti-Semitic speech. And, in the opinion of the leading Jewish organization [in Germany] of that era, no more than 10 percent of the cases were mishandled by the authorities.[2]

The German hate speech laws were enforced even against leading Nazis, some of whom served substantial prison terms. But rather than suppressing the Nazis' anti-Semitic ideology, these prosecutions had the perverse but predictable result of many censorial efforts—amplifying the attention and support that the targeted expression receives. As Danish journalist Flemming Rose reports, for example, between 1923 and 1933, the virulently anti-Semitic newspaper *Der Stürmer*, published by Julius Streicher, "was either confiscated or [its] editors [were] taken to court on . . . thirty-six occasions." Yet, "the more charges Streicher faced, the greater became the admiration of his supporters. The courts became an important platform for Streicher's campaign against the Jews."[3]

This familiar "forbidden fruits" reaction to enforcing hate speech laws against the Nazis prompted opposition to this strategy by Alfred Wiener, a German Jew who dedicated much of his life to documenting antisemitism and Nazi crimes. In 1919, the year when Supreme Court Justice Oliver Wendell Holmes wrote a famous dissent declaring that "the correction of evil counsels" is a better strategy than censoring them,[4] Wiener advocated that very approach toward Nazi speech in Germany. Commenting on the unintended negative consequences of the prosecutions under Germany's hate speech laws, Wiener wrote: "We create martyrs. . . . Enlightenment, that is the solution."[5] Notably, Holmes's dissent was joined by Justice Louis Brandeis, the first Jewish Supreme Court Justice.

The major problem with Germany's response to rising Nazism was not that the Nazis enjoyed too much free speech, but that the Nazis literally got away with murder. In effect, they stole free speech from everyone else, including anti-Nazis, Jews, and other minorities. As Aryeh Neier commented in his classic book about the Skokie case: "The lesson of Germany in the 1920s is that a free society cannot be . . . maintained if it will not act . . . forcefully to punish political violence. It is as if no effort had been made in the United States to punish the murderers of Medgar Evers, Martin Luther King, Jr. . . . and . . . other victims" of violence during the civil rights movement.[6]

The 1994 Rwanda genocide—in which members of the ethnic majority Hutus slaughtered an estimated five hundred thousand to eight hundred thousand members of the Tutsi ethnic minority—is often cited to the same effect as the Holocaust, as allegedly demonstrating that we should punish hateful expression that falls short of what is often called the "emergency" standard under modern US law: when the expression, considered in its overall context, directly causes or imminently threatens certain specific serious harm.

This argument reflects the widespread conventional wisdom that hateful speech about Tutsis had a sufficiently close causal connection to the mass murders, which is captured in Samantha Power's widely quoted soundbite that the killers "carried a machete in one hand and a transistor radio in the other." Power (who was then a war correspondent) was referring to broadcasts by RTLM (Radio Television des Mille Collines), which was owned and controlled by Hutu hard-liners. In fact, though, far from showing that broader hate speech restrictions are needed to prevent discriminatory violence and foster unity, the actual evidence about the Rwandan situation undermines those conclusions.

Much of the expression involved in the Rwandan genocide was punishable under First Amendment standards because it directly, materially contributed to imminent genocidal violence. This expression not only intentionally incited genocide of Tutsis in general, but also provided essential information that facilitated the murders of specific Tutsis. RTLM broadcasts listed the names of particular Tutsis who should be killed, and provided directions to their hiding places. For these reasons, the International Criminal Tribunal for Rwanda (ICTR) convicted RTLM, two of its leaders, and a newspaper editor of international crimes.[7] Moreover, the ICTR found that one of these leaders had ordered the murders of Tutsi civilians.[8] Punishing this kind of expression is fully consistent with First Amendment principles.

But what about other expression, which fell short of intentional incitement or direct facilitation of genocide, but nevertheless conveyed hateful views about Tutsis—which I will designate as "non-emergency" hate speech? Did such expression sufficiently contribute to the genocide such that it should also be punished? The ICTR's Appeals Chamber upheld the conviction of one RTLM principal, Ferdinand Nahimana, on this ground,[9] but one judge dissented from that holding, which also has been criticized by other international human rights experts.[10] The dissenting judge, Theodor Meron, noted that "the Appeals Chamber . . . has marshaled no evidence" that "establish[es] a causal nexus between Nahimana's" expression and the genocide.[11] As I will discuss further below, multiple social scientists and human rights experts have concurred with Judge Meron's conclusion. First, though, I will discuss another important aspect of Judge Meron's dissent, which flagged additional reasons not to punish hate speech except in accordance with the emergency principle.

While deploring Nahimana's "repugnant" hate speech, Judge Meron stressed the negative human rights ramifications of punishing it absent a tight causal connection to the genocide. In particular, Judge Meron noted the negative impact that non-emergency hate speech restrictions would have on the rights of ethnic and political minority groups—ironically, the very kinds of groups who were massacred in the Rwandan genocide. This concern had been raised by a friend-of-the-court brief filed by the Open Society Justice Initiative, an international human rights organization, along with eleven other human rights organizations from multiple countries, all over the world.[12] Judge Meron wrote:

> The reason for protecting hate speech . . . is enabling political opposition, especially in emerging democracies. Amicus curiae . . . has brought to the Tribunal's attention numerous examples of regimes' suppressing criticism by claiming that their opponents were engaged in criminal incitement [through hate speech]. Such efforts at suppression are particularly acute where political parties correspond to ethnic cleavages. . . . Regimes often charge critical journalists and political opponents with . . . "incitement to hatred" . . . . Officials in some countries have explicitly cited the example of RTLM in order to quell criticism of the governing regimes.[13]

Tragically, these general downsides of non-emergency hate speech restrictions have been of increasing concern in Rwanda itself, which passed such laws for the professed purpose of reconciling Rwandans and preventing another catastrophe similar to the 1994 genocide. This legislation, which has been criticized by international human rights organizations, imposes broad, vague restrictions on expression that constitutes "Divisionism" or "Genocide Ideology."[14] A 2016 report by a German foundation, the Friedrich Ebert Stiftung, concluded: "In Rwanda, hate speech legislation has become a tool of repression."[15] A 2010 Amnesty International report documented that this legislation has been "officially interpreted" as punishing, "for example, general opposition to government policies, the support of political candidates who are not part of the governing RPF [the Tutsi-led Rwandan Patriotic Front], calls for prosecution of unpunished RPF war crimes, criticism of the lack of media freedom and comments on the deficiencies of the hate speech laws themselves."[16]

Another counter-productive aspect of Rwanda's non-emergency hate speech restrictions is that, far from countering divisiveness, they actually foster it. Amnesty International has documented that "denunciation" and "false accusations" under the law are used to settle personal and political disputes.[17] Tragically, "many false accusations take place during the genocide commemoration period when tensions are particularly acute."[18] The Friedrich Ebert Stiftung report reached the following conclusion about Rwanda's hate speech laws: "Despite the stated aim to foster unity, the laws are more likely to lead to an even deeper split in an already traumatized society. They have themselves become a tool that fuels further conflict instead of preventing it."[19]

In the years since the 1994 Rwandan genocide, multiple experts have studied the causal factors in general, and the role of RTLM and other expression in particular. While some conclude that expression did play a material contributory role, others disagree, and are highly critical of the ICTR's conclusions on this issue. For example, on the basis of 100 interviews of convicted perpetrators, Rwandan cultural anthropologist Charles Mironko found that many ordinary villagers either did not receive genocidal radio transmissions or did not interpret them as encouraging killing.[20]

Political scientist Scott Straus undertook a quantitative analysis of radio reception and genocidal violence, noting the following flaws in the assumed role that RTLM played: RTLM's coverage at the time was very uneven, especially in rural areas, where it was unable to reach a full 90–95 percent of the population; only 10 percent of the population owned a radio in 1994; the initial violence did not correspond with areas of broadcast coverage; and the most extensive and inflammatory broadcasts came after most of the killings had already taken place.[21] Although Straus acknowledged that RTLM had "marginal and conditional" effects, including likely convincing a small number of people to commit violence, he also concluded that "radio alone cannot account for either the onset of most genocidal violence or the participation of most perpetrators."[22]

One further expert who concluded that RTLM did not incite the genocide is Richard Carver, an expert on Africa who worked for both Amnesty International and Human Rights Watch, who stated that "the massacres would have taken place with or without the RTLM broadcasts."[23]

Prof. Straus has pointed out the following irony: the widespread willingness to attribute Rwandan Hutus' participation in genocide to their purported susceptibility to expression conveying negative stereotypes about Tutsis *itself* reflects negative stereotypes about Rwandan Hutus, or Rwandans in general. He explained: "The Rwandan public is often characterized as hearing a drumbeat of racist messages and directly internalizing them or as hearing orders to kill and heeding the command. Those views are consistent with stereotypes about Rwandans, namely that they obey orders blindly, that they are poorly educated and thus easily manipulated, and that they are immersed in a culture of prejudice."[24]

In sum, the Rwandan situation illustrates that non-emergency hate speech restrictions do more harm than good; they would not clearly prevent a future Rwandan genocide, but they do clearly stifle dissident and minority group speech, while fueling divisiveness.

Greg Lukianoff:

Richard Delgado, an early champion of speech codes and now more famous as a founding scholar in the field of Critical Race Theory, cites the Rwandan genocide, along with Weimar Germany, as cautionary tales against free-speech purism.[25] The problem is that neither historical precedent supports the idea that speech restraints could have prevented a genocide.

Weimar Germany had laws banning hateful speech (particularly hateful speech directed at Jews), and top Nazis including Joseph Goebbels, Theodor Fritsch, and Julius Streicher actually were sentenced to prison time for violating them.[26] The efforts of the Weimar Republic to suppress the speech of the Nazis are so well known in academic circles that one professor has described the idea that speech restrictions would have stopped the Nazis as "the Weimar Fallacy."[27]

A 1922 law passed in response to violent political agitators such as the Nazis permitted Weimar authorities to censor press criticism of the government and advocacy of violence.[28] This was followed by a number of emergency decrees expanding the power to censor newspapers. The Weimar Republic not only shut down hundreds of Nazi newspapers, but it accelerated that crackdown on speech as the Nazis ascended to power.[29] Hitler himself was banned from speaking in several German states from 1925 until 1927.[30]

Far from being an impediment to the spread of National Socialist ideology, Hitler and the Nazis used the attempts to suppress their speech as public relations coups. Party members waved the ban like a bloody shirt to claim they were being targeted for exposing the international conspiracy to suppress "true" Germans. As one poster explained:

> Why is Adolf Hitler not allowed to speak? Because he is ruthless in uncovering the rulers of the German economy, the international bank Jews and their lackeys, the Democrats, Marxists, Jesuits, and Free Masons! Because he wants to free the workers from the domination of big money![31]

Considering that the Nazi movement's core ideology, as espoused by Hitler in *Mein Kampf*, rested on an alleged conspiracy between Jews and their sympathizers in government to politically disempower Aryan Germans, it is not surprising that the Nazis were able to spin government censorship into propaganda victories and seeming confirmation of their claims that they were speaking truth to power, and that power was aligned against them.

Indeed, censorship that was employed ineffectively to stop the rise of the Nazis was a boon to the Nazis when it came to consolidating their power. The laws mentioned earlier that allowed Weimar authorities to shut down newspapers, and additional laws intended to limit the spread of Nazi ideology via the radio, had their reins turned over to the Nazi party when Hitler became chancellor. Predictably, the Nazis used these preexisting means of censorship to crush any political speech opposing them, allowing for an absolute grip on the country that would have been much more difficult or impossible to achieve had there been strong legal protections for press and speech.

So, policing Nazi speech was tried and in fact did not avert the rise of the Nazis. Does that mean there was no way to stop the Nazis? The rise of Hitler and the Nazis wasn't inevitable—there were likely a few historical off-ramps.

Hitler's niece, who had been living with him, and with whom he had been rumored to be in a romantic relationship, was found dead in September 1931 with a gunshot wound in her lung.[32] The death was not seriously investigated before being declared a suicide, but it is not hard to imagine that had this been investigated or become a scandal, it could have stopped Hitler's personal ascent (he was appointed Chancellor in January 1933).

The main and most obvious path that would have averted the rise of the Nazi party would have been the aggressive, or even just proportionate, prosecution of the political violence by the Nazi party before it had seized power.

> "It was a permissive attitude towards violence and the degradation of the rule of law—not a permissive attitude toward free speech—that led to the most notorious atrocity in history."

In 1923, the government of Bavaria banned large public meetings of the Nazi party. In response, inspired by Mussolini's march on Rome, Hitler and over six hundred of his compatriots, including other future leaders of the Nazi party, attempted a violent coup in Munich, involving a firefight that led to the deaths of four police officers and sixteen Nazi party members. Afterward, Hitler was tried and convicted for high treason.[33]

For the crime of a deadly attempted overthrow of the government, Hitler was given the absurdly lenient sentence of only five years[34]—of which he served a total of eight months, during which he wrote *Mein Kampf* before being released on good behavior.[35] The only other person sentenced for the coup, Rudolf Hess, was also sentenced to five years and, like Hitler, only served eight months. Similarly, other instances of political violence committed by Nazis went under-punished when they were punished at all, owing to the sympathy afforded to them by judges and juries that was not afforded to their leftist and communist counterparts.

It should not require the benefit of hindsight to understand that this was a grave error. For leading a deadly attempted overthrow of the government, by the standards of the time, Hitler could have been executed, given life in prison, or at the very least, permanently banned from holding public office.

In sum, restrictions on speech failed to stop the Nazis and ultimately proved to be strong weapons in their hands. It was a permissive attitude towards violence and the degradation of the rule of law—not a permissive attitude toward free speech—that led to the most notorious atrocity in history.

In the case of the Rwandan genocide, the problem wasn't excessive commitment to free speech, but rather a government-led criminal conspiracy to commit genocide, and the infamous genocidal radio broadcasts would not have amounted to protected speech. Here are two key points missed by those who blame the Rwandan genocide on free speech.

The speech at issue during the Rwandan genocide would have been unprotected in virtually any country in the world. Even in the US, it would have met the test for unprotected incitement. The First Amendment and its associated case law are the strongest legal codification of the freedom of expression in the world today. Even so, the Supreme Court has defined several narrow limits on the freedom of expression, including for defamation,[36] fighting words,[37] obscenity,[38] harassment,[39] and true threats.[40] In the United States, since the 1969 Supreme Court decision, *Brandenburg v. Ohio*, speech advocating a crime loses constitutional protection when it is 1) directed at producing imminent lawless action, and 2) likely to produce such action.[41]

Radio broadcasts during the Rwandan genocide, which frequently included names, addresses, and current locations of Tutsis, encouraged and provided the means for murders, easily clearing the Brandenburg test.[42] Rwandan speech wasn't free to begin with: Radio stations were not permitted to operate if the government disagreed with their viewpoints and, once the genocide started, both the official state radio station and its nominal opponents were directly controlled by pro-government forces.[43] To use the authorized media of a genocidal state as evidence of the danger posed by excessive liberty suggests a failure to understand the core concept of liberty.

Like many anti-free speech stances, the claim that too much free speech caused the Rwandan genocide shows a bizarrely unrealistic understanding of politics and political power. Murder, especially indiscriminate mass murder, was illegal in Rwanda, but illegality does not matter when the government and police are controlled by those who have no regard for the law. Put simply, if the government would not enforce laws against murdering Tutsis, there is simply no reason to believe it would have enforced laws against hate speech targeting Tutsis. As was the case with Nazi Germany, the proximal issue was not speech, but state-sanctioned mass murder.

A recurrent bad argument against freedom of speech involves a kind of magical thinking by which the passage of a speech restriction eliminates a problem, without realizing that any law has to be passed and enforced by actual people. I call this view "naive statism." Those who believe that hate speech laws would have prevented the rise of the Nazis in Weimar Germany tend to ignore the fact that the existing hate speech limitations were enforced by people who voted for Nazis in large numbers and by judges who refused to seriously punish people like Hitler, even for multiple murders and an attempted coup. In Rwanda, the naive statism argument for censorship laws ignores the fact that the Rwandan genocide was, of course, illegal even by Rwandan law.

If those in charge of the government are orchestrating a genocide, a law banning hate speech is a silly, dismissible barrier—a shield as thick and sturdy as the parchment it's written on.

Further Reading

For more on the application, history, and urgency of free speech, the authors have prepared a reading list you can visit at https://www.thefire.org/research-learn/war-on-words.

Author Biographies

Greg Lukianoff is an attorney, *New York Times* best-selling author, and the President and CEO of the Foundation for Individual Rights and Expression (FIRE). He is the author of several books, including *Unlearning Liberty: Campus Censorship and the End of American Debate* (2012), and he co-authored *The Coddling of the American Mind: How Good Intentions and Bad Ideas Are Setting Up a Generation for Failure* (2018) with Jonathan Haidt, and *The Canceling of the American Mind: Cancel Culture Undermines Trust and Threatens Us All—But There Is a Solution* (2023) with Rikki Schlott. Greg is also an Executive Producer of *Can We Take a Joke?* (2015), a feature-length documentary that explores the collision between comedy, censorship, and outrage culture, and of *Mighty Ira: A Civil Liberties Story* (2020), an award-winning feature-length film about the life and career of former ACLU Executive Director Ira Glasser.

Nadine Strossen is the John Marshall Harlan II Professor of Law Emerita at New York Law School and was the national President of the American Civil Liberties Union from 1991 to 2008. With more than forty years of experience in First Amendment law, Strossen is a leading expert and frequent speaker/media commentator on constitutional law and civil liberties, who has testified before Congress on multiple occasions. She serves on the advisory boards of the ACLU, Academic Freedom Alliance, Heterodox Academy, and National Coalition Against Censorship. Strossen is the author of several books, including *HATE: Why We Should Resist It with Free Speech, Not Censorship* (2018) and *Free Speech: What Everyone Needs to Know®* (2023). Her many honorary degrees and awards include the American Bar Association's Margaret Brent Women Lawyers of Achievement Award (2017), and in 2023, the National Coalition Against Censorship selected Strossen for its Lifetime Achievement Award for Free Speech.

Jacob Mchangama is the Founder and Executive Director of The Future of Free Speech and a research professor at Vanderbilt University. He is the recipient of numerous awards for his work on free speech and human rights and has commented extensively on these topics in outlets including the *Washington Post*, *Wall Street Journal*, *The Economist*, *Foreign Affairs* and *Foreign Policy*. He is also the author of the critically acclaimed book *Free Speech: A History From Socrates to Social Media.*

Notes

Foreword by Jacob Mchangama

1 Jacob Mchangama, *Free Speech: A History from Socrates to Social Media* (Basic Books, 2022), 426 (kindle edition).

2 Ibid. at 137.

3 Ibid. at 283.

4 Union of Soviet Socialist Republics. *Constitution (Fundamental Law) of the Union of Soviet Socialist Republics*. December 5, 1936. Accessed March 27, 2025. https://www.marxists.org/reference/archive/stalin/works/1936/12/05.htm.

5 For an example of this in practice, see Sean O'Toole, "The lasting impact of banned apartheid book, 'House of Bondage'," *The* (Johannesburg) *Sunday Times*, March 21, 2021, https://www.timeslive.co.za/sunday-times/lifestyle/2021–03-21-the-lasting-impact-of-banned-apartheid-book-house-of-bondage/.

6 Karl Marx, "On Freedom of the Press." *Rheinische Zeitung*, no. 135, suppl., May 15, 1842.

7 Mchangama, 228 to 230 (kindle edition).

8 Skaaning, Svend-Erik, and Suthan Krishnarajan. "Who In The World Supports Free Speech? Findings from A Global Survey." *The Future of Free Speech*, March 17, 2025. https://futurefreespeech.org/who-supports-free-speech-findings-from-a-global-survey/.

9 Mary Anne Franks, *Fearless Speech: Breaking Free from the First Amendment* (Bold Type Books, 2024), 17.

10 James Madison, "Report on the Virginia Resolutions," 1800.

11 Elie Luzac, "An Essay on Freedom of Expression," 1749.

Argument #1: Words Are Violence

1 David Hudson, "80 years ago the Supreme Court introduced 'Fighting Words,'" *FIRE*, Mar. 9, 2022, https://www.thefire.org/news/80-years-ago-supreme-court-introduced-fighting-words.

2 *Gitlow v. New York*, 268 U.S. 652, 673 (1925) (Holmes, J., dissenting).

3 David Cole, "Why We Must Still Defend Free Speech," *New York Review*, Sept. 8, 2017, https://www.nybooks.com/articles/2017/09/28/why-we-must-still-defend-free-speech/?lp_txn_id=1273809.

4 *See generally* "Quote Origin: The Man Who First Flung a Word of Abuse at His Enemy Instead of a Spear Was the Founder of Civilization," quoteinvestigator.com, Aug. 5, 2015, https://quoteinvestigator.com/2015/08/05/spear/.

5 "Updated Statement on Violent Protest at University of California, Berkeley," *FIRE*, February 2, 2017, https://www.thefire.org/news/updated-statement-violent-protest-university-california-berkeley.

6 Ryne Weiss, "UC Berkeley Chancellor Condemns Calls for Violence, Reiterates Support for Free Speech," *FIRE*, February 17, 2017, https://www.thefire.org/news/uc-berkeley-chancellor-condemns-calls-violence-reiterates-support-free-speech ("On February 7, *The Daily Californian* published five op-eds, in the editor's words, 'in favor of the use of violence in protests,' with titles such as 'Violence helped ensure safety of students,' 'Black bloc did what campus should have,' and 'Condemning protesters same as condoning hate speech.'").

7 Lisa Feldman Barrett, "When Is Speech Violence?," *New York Times*, July 14, 2017, https://www.nytimes.com/2017/07/14/opinion/sunday/when-is-speech-violence.html.

8 For more, see Jonathan Haidt and Greg Lukianoff, "Why It's a Bad Idea to Tell Students Words are Violence," *The Atlantic*, July 18, 2017, https://www.theatlantic.com/education/archive/2017/07/why-its-a-bad-idea-to-tell-students-words-are-violence/533970/.

Argument #2: Words Are Dangerous

1 *Whitney v. California*, 274 U.S. 357, 377 (1927) (Brandeis, J., concurring).

2 Thurman Hart, "Abolitionists and Free Speech," *Free Speech Center at Middle Tennessee State University*, updated January 9, 2025, https://firstamendment.mtsu.edu/article/abolitionists-and-free-speech/ ("In response to the overwhelming submission of petitions to the US House of Representatives in support of abolitionist legislation, pro-slavery and moderate anti-slavery forces banded together to pass a gag rule in the House.").

3 "Woman Suffrage and the 19th Amendment," *National Archives*, visited March 24, 2025.

4 E.g., *Schenck v. United States*, 249 U.S. 47 (1919) (upholding a conviction under the Espionage Act for mailing material opposing the draft).

5 "Collective Bargaining and Civil Liberties," *ACLU*, March 25, 2011, https://www.aclu.org/documents/collective-bargaining-and-civil-liberties.

6 "On this day, massive raids during the Red Scare," *National Constitution Center*, January 2, 2024, https://constitutioncenter.org/blog/on-this-day-massive-raids-during-the-red-scare.

7 Ibid. Also see Erick Trickey, "When America's Most Prominent Socialist Was Jailed for Speaking Out Against World War I," *Smithsonian Magazine*, June 15, 2018, https://www.smithsonianmag.com/history/fiery-socialist-challenged-nations-role-wwi-180969386/.

8 Mycah Hazel, "They marched for desegregation—then they disappeared for 45 days," *NPR*, July 19 2023, https://www.npr.org/2023/07/19/1150083525/they-marched-for-desegregation-then-they-disappeared-for-45-days.

9 Leigh Ann Wheeler, "The Making of the Right to Abortion," *ACLU*, October 2, 2019, https://www.aclu.org/news/reproductive-freedom/the-making-of-the-right-to-abortion.

10 Adkins, Judith. ""These People Are Frightened to Death": Congressional Investigations and the Lavender Scare." *Prologue Magazine* 48, no. 2 (Summer 2016). https://www.archives.gov/publications/prologue/2016/summer/lavender.html.

11 Greg Lukianoff, *Unlearning Liberty: Campus Censorship and the End of American Debate* (Encounter Books, 2014).

12 *Terminiello v. Chicago*, 337 U.S. 1, 4 (1949).

13 *See generally* "Freedom of Speech," FIRE, https://www.thefire.org/research-learn/freedom-speech.

14 *See generally* Greg Lukianoff and Ryne Weiss, "Fleabag, Noom, the Future of Freedom, & 'Censorship Gravity'," FIRE, Oct. 19, 2020, https://www.thefire.org/news/blogs/eternally-radical-idea/fleabag-noom-future-freedom-censorship-gravity.

15 For more, see Eric Berkowitz, *Dangerous Ideas: A Brief History of Censorship in the West, from the Ancients to Fake News* (Beacon Press, 2021).

Argument #3: Hate Speech Isn't Free Speech

1 *See generally* Nadine Strossen, *HATE: Why We Should Resist It with Free Speech, Not Censorship* (Oxford University Press, 2018).

2 *See generally* "Is Hate Speech Legal?", *FIRE*, https://www.thefire.org/research-learn/hate-speech-legal.

3 Ibid.

4 "Rudy Giuliani slams New York City major Bill de Blasio, black lives matter organization," *Fox News*, July 10, 2020,

https://www.foxnews.com/transcript/rudy-giuliani-slams-new-york-city-mayor-bill-de-blasio-black-lives-matter-organization (Giuliani called BLM "a racist organization" that is "actually participating in hate speech").

5 "ADL Debunk: Disinformation and the BLM Protests," *ADL*, July 21, 2020, https://www.adl.org/resources/report/adl-debunk-disinformation-and-blm-protests?gad_source=1&gclid=Cj0KCQjw16O_BhDNARIsAC3i2GB0TBy4eSFFGMd-itWDZE8LqIpSj7HEnm8kymsPvZtvjV2rWHgZubIaAl4EEALw_wcB&gclsrc=aw.ds (critiques "hate-based disinformation campaigns around the ongoing Black Lives Matter demonstrations").

6 See, e.g., Strossen, *HATE: Why We Should Resist It with Free Speech, Not Censorship* at 78 (describing a Canadian case in which a man was charged with illegal hate speech for distributing four flyers, in which the four different courts that ruled on the case reached three different conclusions as to which, if any, of the flyers did in fact constitute illegal hate speech).

7 As cited in testimony of Nadine Strossen, U.S. Senate Committee on Health, Education, Labor, and Pensions. *Exploring Free Speech on College Campuses*. S. Hrg. 115–660. 115th Cong., 1st sess., October 26, 2017, https://www.govinfo.gov/content/pkg/CHRG-115shrg27450/html/CHRG-115shrg27450.htm.

8 *See* Greg Lukianoff and Ryne Weiss, "The *NY Post* & Twitter Crash Into 'The Streisand Effect,' 'Censorship Envy,' and 'the Slippery Slope Tendency'," *FIRE*, Oct. 15, 2020, https://www.thefire.org/news/blogs/eternally-radical-idea/nypost-twitter-crash-streisand-effect-censorship-envy-and.

9 Southern Poverty Law Center, *The Alt-Right on Campus: What Students Need to Know* (Southern Poverty Law Center, 2017) https://www.splcenter.org/wp-content/uploads/files/soc_alt-right_campus_guide_2017_web.pdf at p. 5 ("When an alt-right personality is scheduled to speak on campus, the

most effective course of action is to deprive the speaker of the thing he or she wants most—a spectacle. Alt-right personalities know their cause is helped by news footage of large jeering crowds, heated confrontations and outright violence at their events. It allows them to play the victim and gives them a larger platform for their racist message.").

10 "Life After Hate: A Former White Power Leader Redeems Himself," *America's Black Holocaust Museum*, accessed March 31, 2025, https://www.abhmuseum.org/life-after-hate-a-former-white-power-leader-redeems-himself/.

11 *ECRI General Policy Recommendation No. 15 on Combatting Hate Speech* (European Commission Against Racism and Intolerance, adopted December 8, 2015), 13, https://www.coe.int/en/web/european-commission-against-racism-and-intolerance/recommendation-no.15

12 "The ADL Global 100: Index of Antisemitism," ADL, https://www.adl.org/adl-global-100-index-antisemitism (last visited Jan 21, 2025).

13 *See* "Loi n° 90–615 du 13 juillet 1990 tendant à réprimer tout acte raciste, antisémite ou xénophobe," (Jul. 14, 1990), *available at* http://www.legifrance.gouv.fr/WAspad/UnTexteDeJorf?numjo=JUSX9010223L (Gayssot Act) *and* "The ADL Global 100: Index of Antisemitism," ADL, https://www.adl.org/adl-global-100-index-antisemitism (last visited Jan 21, 2025).

14 Ibid.

15 "Public Order Act 1986," legislation.gov.uk, https://www.legislation.gov.uk/ukpga/1986/64/contents (last visited Jan 21, 2025).

16 Jennifer Rubin *et al.*, "Intolerance in Western Europe: Analysis of trends and associated factors," RAND, Jan. 27, 2014, p. 65, *available at* https://www.rand.org/pubs/research_reports/RR334.html.

17 Dan Glaun, "Germany's Laws on Hate Speech, Nazi Propaganda & Holocaust Denial: An Explainer," *Frontline*, July 1, 2021, https://www.pbs.org/wgbh/frontline/article/germanys-laws-antisemitic-hate-speech-nazi-propaganda-holocaust-denial/.

18 *See* "Intolerance toward Muslims in Germany growing, survey finds," *Daily Sabah*, Jul. 13, 2019, https://www.dailysabah.com/islamophobia/2019/07/13/intolerance-toward-muslims-in-germany-growing-survey-finds (Islamophobia) *and* "Anti-Semitism 'sharply rising' in Germany," *Deutsche Welle*, Sept. 10, 2020, https://www.dw.com/en/anti-semitism-in-germany-sharply-rising-warns-security-agency/a-55211350 (anti-Semitism).

19 *See generally* Cass R. Sunstein, *Going to Extremes: How Like Minds Unite and Divide* (Oxford University Press, reprinted 2011).

20 In Wisconsin v. Mitchell, 508 U.S. 476 (1993), the Supreme Court rejected a First Amendment challenge to this type of law, although the Wisconsin Supreme Court had struck it down under the First Amendment. First Amendment experts likewise disagree on this issue.

21 Jenny Goldsberry, "Calgary's Black Lives Matter president charged with hate crime," *Washington Examiner*, June 15, 2023, https://www.washingtonexaminer.com/news/2238837/calgarys-black-lives-matter-president-charged-with-hate-crime/.

22 Kevin Martin, "Crown withdraws hate-crime allegation against Calgary Black Lives Matter president," *Calgary Herald*, June 16, 2023, https://calgaryherald.com/news/crime/charges-against-calgary-black-lives-matter-president-dropped.

23 Ashitha Nagesh, "How woman with coconut placard was tracked down, taken to court–and acquitted," *BBC*, September 14, 2024, https://www.bbc.com/news/articles/cvgwew5v4qyo.

24 Jake Offenhartz, "NYC journalist who documented pro-Palestinian vandalism arrested on felony hate crime charges," *Associated Press*, August 6, 2024, https://apnews.com/article/gaza-nypd-sam-seligson-brooklyn-museum-eea8ee12248d38d856fe5cabcac7a0d1.

25 "Independent videographer thrown to ground, arrested at NYC protest," US Press Freedom Tracker, updated August 7, 2024, https://pressfreedomtracker.us/all-incidents/independent-videographer-thrown-to-ground-arrested-at-nyc-protest/.

26 Aaron Sibarium, "Inside State-Run 'Bias-Response Hotlines,' Where Fellow Citizens Can Report Your 'Offensive Joke'," *The Washington Free Beacon*, January 22, 2025, https://freebeacon.com/policy/inside-state-run-bias-response-hotlines-where-fellow-citizens-can-report-your-offensive-joke/.

27 Ibid.

28 Ibid.

29 Christian Schneider, "'Bias Teams Welcome the Class of 1984," *The Wall Street Journal*, August 5, 2019, https://www.wsj.com/articles/bias-teams-welcome-the-class-of-1984–11565045215.

30 Brooke Erin Duffy and Colten Meisner. "Platform governance at the margins: Social media creators' experiences with algorithmic (in)visibilty." *Media, Culture, and Society* 45, Issue 2 (2022), 9. ("Participants discussed the human agency of not only *platform* representatives, but also fellow *users* who allegedly "reported" content as a retaliatory practice.").

31 Liz Wolfe, "Bias Response Teams Thwarted in Their Goal of a Sensitive Campus by the First Amendment," *Reason*, October 23, 2027, https://reason.com/2017/10/23/bias-response-teams-thwarted-in-their-go/.

32 Ibid.

Argument #4: About Shoutdowns

1 S.T. Stevens, *2025 College Free Speech Rankings: What Is the State of Free Speech on America's College Campuses?* (FIRE, 2024), https://www.thefire.org/research-learn/2025-college-free-speech-rankings ("This year, just over half of students (52 percent) reported that blocking other students from attending a campus speech is at least "rarely" acceptable, up from 45 percent in 2023 and 37 percent in 2022. Even more concerning, about a third of students (32 percent) reported that using violence to stop a campus speech is at least "rarely" acceptable, up from 27 percent last year and 20 percent in 2022.").

2 Spence v. Washington, 418 U.S. 405, 410–11 (1974).

3 340 U.S. 315 (1951).

4 *Edwards v. South Carolina*, 372 U.S. 229 (1963).

5 Ibid. at 328 (Black, J., dissenting).

6 Adam Steinbaugh, "Hecklers shout down California attorney general, assembly majority leader at Whittier College," *FIRE*, October 13, 2017, https://www.thefire.org/news/hecklers-shout-down-california-attorney-general-assembly-majority-leader-whittier-college; Sabrina Conza and Alex Morey, "Stanford Law students shout down 5th Circuit judge: A post-mortem," *FIRE*, March 13, 2023, https://www.thefire.org/news/stanford-law-students-shout-down-5th-circuit-judge-post-mortem.

7 Zach Greenberg, "UC Hastings, University of North Texas can pave the way for free speech by addressing the 'heckler' veto'," *FIRE*, March 4, 2022, https://www.thefire.org/news/uc-hastings-university-north-texas-can-pave-way-free-speech-addressing-hecklers-veto.

8 Ibid.

9 David Lat (@DavidLat), "1/ THREAD. I have appended an update/correction to my Original Jurisdiction post from yesterday about the March 10 protest at Yale Law School. The disruption was much worse than I originally

reported. Here's the text of my update on @YaleLawSch," Twitter (now X), March 18, 2022, https://x.com/DavidLat/status/1504841221772034058.

10 Adam Steinbaugh, "CSU Los Angeles President Fails to Prevent Shapiro Talk, But Protesters Try Their Hardest Anyway," *FIRE*, February 26, 2016, https://www.thefire.org/news/csu-los-angeles-president-fails-prevent-shapiro-talk-protesters-try-their-hardest-anyway ("Once Shapiro actually began speaking, a fire alarm began blaring.").

11 "Campus police no match for heckler with cowbell who hijacked speech at Portland State," *FIRE*, March 12, 2019, https://www.thefire.org/news/campus-police-no-match-heckler-cowbell-who-hijacked-speech-portland-state.

12 See, e.g., *Lamont v. Postmaster General*, 381 U.S. 301 (1965).

13 *Kleindienst v. Mandel*, 408 U.S. 753, 775 (1972) (Marshall, J., dissenting). The majority based its ruling on other issues in the case, which is why Marshall's opinion was a dissent.

14 Frederick Douglass, "A plea for free speech in Boston," 1860, available online at https://constitutioncenter.org/the-constitution/historic-document-library/detail/frederick-douglass-a-plea-for-free-speech-in-boston-1860.

15 See Andrew Kirell, "Anti-'Amnesty' Activists Shout Down Dem Rep. Gutiérrez with 'USA!' Chant During Spanish-Language Event," *MEDIAite*, March 26, 2015 3:22 PM, https://www.mediaite.com/tv/anti-amnesty-activists-shout-down-dem-rep-gutierrez-with-usa-chant-during-spanish-language-event/ and Bill Vann, "Hecklers shout down journalist's antiwar speech at college commencement," *World Socialist Web Site*, May 23, 2003, https://www.wsws.org/en/articles/2003/05/hedg-m23.html.

16 Sabrina Conza and Alex Morey, "Stanford Law students shout down 5th Circuit judge: A post-mortem," *FIRE*, March 13, 2023, https://www.thefire.org/news/stanford-law-students-shout-down-5th-circuit-judge-post-mortem.

Argument #5: Free Speech Is Outdated

1 *See, e.g.*, Ivory Coast Constitution of 2016, art. 19, https://www.constituteproject.org/constitution/Cote_DIvoire_2016.

2 Universal Declaration of Human Rights, G.A. Res. 217A (III), U.N. Doc. A/810 at 71 (1948).

3 International Covenant on Civil and Political Rights, Dec. 16, 1966, 999 U.N.T.S. 171, art. 9.2, entered into force Mar. 23, 1976.

4 Convention for the Protection of Human Rights and Fundamental Freedoms, art. 10, Nov. 4, 1950, 213 U.N.T.S. 221, entered into force Sept. 3, 1953.

5 American Convention on Human Rights, art. 13, Nov. 22, 1969, 1144 U.N.T.S. 123, entered into force July 18, 1978.

6 African Charter on Human and Peoples' Rights, art. 9, June 27, 1981, 1520 U.N.T.S. 217, entered into force Oct. 21, 1986.

7 Ruhollah Khomeini, Fatwa against Salman Rushdie, February 14, 1989, Iran Data Portal, accessed March 18, 2025, https://irandataportal.syr.edu/fatwa-against-salman-rushdie.

8 Bill Hutchinson, "Salman Rushdie speaks of stabbing that almost claimed his life: 'Taking power back'," *ABC News*, April 15, 2024, https://abcnews.go.com/US/salman-rushdie-speaks-stabbing-claimed-life-taking-power/story?id=109234123.

9 "Excerpts From Rushdie's Address: 1,000 Days 'Trapped Inside a Metaphor'," *New York Times*, December 12, 1991, https://www.nytimes.com/1991/12/12/nyregion/excerpts-from-rushdie-s-address-1000-days-trapped-inside-a-metaphor.html.

10 Scott Simon, "Remembering Liu Xiaobo, Who Fought For Human Rights In China," *NPR*, July 15, 2017, https://www.npr.org/transcripts/537311241.

11 Jacob Mchangama, *Free Speech: A History from Socrates to Social Media* (Basic Books, 2022).

12 Gale Holland, Richard Winton and Joe Mozingo, "Hundreds were arrested for peacefully protesting. Here are their stories," *Los Angeles Times*, June 9, 2020, https://www.latimes.com/california/story/2020–06-09/hundreds-were-arrested-for-peacefully-protesting-here-are-their-stories.

13 Courtney Douglas, "Amid Black Lives Matter protests, a crushing moment for journalists facing record attacks, arrests at the hands of law enforcement," *Reporters Committee for Freedom of the Press*, September 4, 2020, https://www.rcfp.org/black-lives-matter-press-freedom/.

14 National Lawyers Guild, "Police Targeting NLG Legal Observers at Black Lives Matter Protests," news release, June 7, 2020, https://www.nlg.org/police-targeting-nlg-legal-observers-at-black-lives-matter-protests/.

15 *Garrison v. Louisiana*, 379 U.S. 64, 74–75 (1964).

16 *United States v. Playboy Ent. Grp., Inc.*, 529 U.S. 803, 818 (2000).

17 *Ashcroft v. Free Speech Coalition*, 535 U.S. 234, 253 (2002).

18 Nat Hentoff, *Free Speech For Me—But Not For Thee* (HarperCollins, 1992), 1.

19 Jacob Mchangama, *Free Speech: A History from Socrates to Social Media* (Basic Books, 2022).

20 *Gitlow v. New York*, 268 U.S. 652 (1925) (holding that the First Amendment bound state and local governments, which had been carrying out much of the censorship).

21 Michael Kent Curtis, *The Curious History of Attempts to Suppress Antislavery Speech, Press, and Petition in 1835–37*, 89 Nw. U. L. Rev. 785, 847 (1995), *available at* https://wakespace.lib.wfu.edu/bitstream/handle/10339/16046/Curtis%20Curious%20History%20of%20Attempts%20to%20Suppress%20Antislavery%20Speech%2c%20Press%2c%20and%20Petition%20in%201835—37.pdf (in support of barring anti-slavery petitions from Congress, Calhoun argued that "They contained reflections injurious to the feelings of himself, and those with whom he was connected,").

22 Aryeh Neier, *Defending My Enemy: American Nazis, the Skokie Case, and the Risks of Freedom*, (The New Press, 2025 edition), afterword by Nadine Strossen, 167–72; see also Angel Eduardo, "Tolerating Intolerance: The Free Speech Paradox," *Quillette*, August 31, 2023, https://quillette.com/2023/08/31/tolerating-intolerance-the-free-speech-paradox/.

23 Jimmy Drennan, "Bad Ideas Have No Rank: The Moral Imperative of Dissent in the Navy," *United States Naval Institute*, July 2019, https://www.usni.org/magazines/proceedings/2019/july/bad-ideas-have-no-rank-moral-imperative-dissent-navy ("Aviators refer to not voicing one's concerns in the cockpit as 'sandbagging' and explicitly forbid it."); Lindsey M. Sprecher, Sarah D. Harris, Elizabeth K. Kim, and Taryn S. Taylor. "Challenging Authority and Speaking Up in the Operating Room Environment: A Narrative Synthesis." *Anaesthesia* 74, no. 7 (2019): 910–922. https://www.sciencedirect.com/science/article/pii/S0007091218312819.

24 Greg Lukianoff, "Mill's (Invincible) Trident: An argument every fan (or opponent) of free speech must know," *FIRE*, February 16, 2021, https://www.thefire.org/news/blogs/eternally-radical-idea/mills-invincible-trident-argument-every-fan-or-opponent-free.

25 For example, see Kelvin Chan, Barbara Ortutay and Nicholas Riccardi, "Meta eliminates fact-checking in latest bow to Trump," *AP*, January 7, 2025, https://apnews.com/article/meta-facts-trump-musk-community-notes-413b8495939a058ff2d25fd23f2e0f43.

26 Matthew Field, "Five times Facebook's fact-checking went wrong," *The Telegraph*, January 7, 2025, https://www.telegraph.co.uk/business/2025/01/07/five-times-facebooks-fact-checkers-wrong/.

27 Loreben Tuquero, "Grok said Biden rescinded a Medal of Freedom from 'Trump's campaign manager.' That's Pants on

Fire!," *Politifact*, January 7, 2025, https://www.politifact.com/factchecks/2025/jan/07/grok-ai/grok-said-biden-rescinded-a-medal-of-freedom-from/.

28 David Moschella, "We Shouldn't Ask Technologists To Be Arbiters of 'Truth'," *Information Technology & Innovation Foundation*, July 5, 2023, https://itif.org/publications/2023/07/05/we-shouldnt-ask-technologists-to-be-arbiters-of-truth/.

29 *FIRE Report on Social Media* (FIRE, 2024), https://www.thefire.org/research-learn/fire-report-social-media-2024.

30 Greg Lukianoff (@glukianoff), "Glad @Meta is moving to community-driven fact-checking. Fact checkers, both on and off campus, have rightfully lost public trust, making this shift entirely predictable. A distributed system can still argue from authority, but won't be beholden just to the popular consensus in Palo Alto, as if it were indistinguishable from truth itself. https://x.com/TheFIREorg/status/1876662977203507566," X quote-post, January 7, 2025, https://x.com/glukianoff/status/1876674236640588072.

Argument #6: Free Speech Is Right-wing

1 Perhaps most famously, Nat Hentoff. Nat Hentoff, *Free Speech For Me—But Not For Thee* (HarperCollins, 1992).

2 *United States v. Schwimmer*, 279 U.S. 644, 654–55 (1929) ("[I]f there is any principle of the Constitution that more imperatively calls for attachment than any other it is the principle of free thought—not free thought for those who agree with us but freedom for the thought that we hate.") (Holmes, J., dissenting).

3 Emerson J. Sykes, "In Defense of *Brandenburg*: The ACLU and Incitement Doctrine in 1919, 1969, and 2019," *Brooklyn Law Review* 85, Issue 1 (2019): 15–36, https://brooklynworks.brooklaw.edu/cgi/viewcontent.cgi?article=2220&context=blr, at 17.

4 600 U.S. 570 (2023).

5 602 U.S. 175 (2024).

6 See, e.g., New York Civil Liberties Union, "NYCLU Statement on ACLU Representation of the NRA at the Supreme Court," Press release, December 9, 2023, https://www.nyclu.org/press-release/nyclu-statement-aclu-representation-nra-supreme-court.

7 American Civil Liberties Union, "Why is the ACLU Representing the NRA Before the U.S. Supreme Court?" *ACLU News*, March 18, 2024, https://www.aclu.org/news/free-speech/why-is-the-aclu-representing-the-nra-before-the-us-supreme-court.

8 Kristen Waggoner and Nadine Strossen, "Web Designer's Free Speech Supreme Court Victory Is a Win for All," *Bloomberg Law*, July 10, 2023, https://news.bloomberglaw.com/us-law-week/web-designers-free-speech-supreme-court-victory-is-a-win-for-all.

9 "The Three Arguments in Support of Free Speech," *FIRE*, accessed February 18, 2025, https://www.thefire.org/research-learn/three-arguments-support-free-speech.

10 Greg Lukianoff, "What is the Eternally Radical Idea?," *FIRE*, April 9, 2020, https://www.thefire.org/news/blogs/eternally-radical-idea/what-eternally-radical-idea.

11 For examples, see Andrew Doyle, "The Democrat plan to censor America," *UnHerd*, October 22, 2024, https://unherd.com/2024/10/how-the-democrats-will-censor-america/, and Anthony L. Fisher, "Why Americans shouldn't buy Trump and Vance's free speech warrior acts," *MSNBC*, July 27, 2024, https://www.msnbc.com/opinion/msnbc-opinion/trump-vance-free-speech-phonies-first-amendment-rcna163102.

12 Greg Lukianoff, "Welcome to the Eternally Radical Idea!," *Eternally Radical Idea*, September 22, 2023, https://eternallyradicalidea.com/p/welcome-to-the-eternally-radical.

13 Greg Lukianoff and Rikki Schlott, *The Canceling of the American Mind* (Simon & Schuster, 2023), ch. 6.

14 Ibid. at ch. 8.

15 Kat Rosenfield (@katrosenfield), "dude, 'fashcasting' is clearly your best if not only option here and it's not even on the list," X (formerly Twitter) reply, June 11, 2024, https://x.com/katrosenfield/status/1800662521155870768.

16 Greg Lukianoff, "Towards a 'More Perfect' Rhetorical Fortress!," *Eternally Radical Idea*, June 11, 2024, https://eternallyradicalidea.com/p/towards-a-more-perfect-rhetorical.

17 Elliot Ackerman et al., "Letter on Justice and Open Debate," *Harper's Magazine*, July 7, 2020, https://harpers.org/a-letter-on-justice-and-open-debate/.

Argument #7: About That Crowded Theater and the Marketplace of Ideas . . .

1 Zeynep Tufecki, "Opinion: We Were Badly Misled About the Event That Changed Our Lives," *New York Times*, March 16, 2025, https://www.nytimes.com/2025/03/16/opinion/covid-pandemic-lab-leak.html.

2 Charles H. Calisher et al., "Statement in Support of the Scientists, Public Health Professionals, and Medical Professionals of China Combatting COVID-19," *The Lancet* 395, no. 10226 (February 19, 2020): e42–e43, https://doi.org/10.1016/S0140–6736(20)30418–9.

3 Lindsey Ellefson, "NY *Times* COVID Reporter Deletes Tweet Claiming 'Racist Roots' of 'Lab Leak Theory' After Backlash," *The Wrap*, May 27, 2021, https://www.thewrap.com/new-york-times-covid-lab-leak-apoorva-mandavilli/. *See also* Ibid. ("Conspiracy theories do nothing but create fear, rumours, and prejudice that jeopardise our global collaboration in the fight against this virus.").

4 Paul Farhi and Jeremy Barr. "The media called the 'lab leak' story a 'conspiracy theory.' Now it's prompted corrections—

and serious new reporting.," *Washington Post*, June 10, 2021, https://www.washingtonpost.com/lifestyle/media/the-media-called-the-lab-leak-story-a-conspiracy-theory-now-its-prompted-corrections—and-serious-new-reporting/2021/06/10/c93972e6-c7b2–11eb-a11b-6c6191ccd599_story.html (outlining how *New York Times* declined to publish Donald G. McNeil Jr.'s story about the lab leak theory).

5 Jackson Sinnenberg, "New Twitter files allege platform suppressed medical opinions, information on COVID," *CBS Austin*, December 28, 2022, https://cbsaustin.com/news/nation-world/new-twitter-files-alleges-platform-suppressed-medical-opinions-information-on-covid-elon-musk-misinformation-cenorship-great-barrington-declaration-vaccines-children-herd-immunity-donald-trump-hunter-biden-president-joe-biden-content-moderation.

6 Katherine Eban, "The Lab-Leak Theory: Inside the Fight to Uncover COVID-19's Origins," *Vanity Fair*, June 3, 2021, https://www.vanityfair.com/news/2021/06/the-lab-leak-theory-inside-the-fight-to-uncover-covid-19s-origins ("In late March, former Centers for Disease Control director Robert Redfield received death threats from fellow scientists after telling CNN that he believed COVID-19 had originated in a lab. "I was threatened and ostracized because I proposed another hypothesis," Redfield told *Vanity Fair*.").

7 Sheryl Gay Stolberg and Benjamin Mueller, "Lab Leak or Not? How Politics Shaped the Battle Over Covid's Origin," *New York Times*, March 19, 2023, https://www.nytimes.com/2023/03/19/us/politics/covid-origins-lab-leak-politics.html (describing how a Stanford microbiologist's Spring 2021 request to his congresswoman led to Rep. Anna Eshoo becoming "one of the first Democrats in Congress to call for an investigation into the origins of Covid").

8 Julian E. Barnes, "C.I.A. Now Favors Lab Leak Theory to Explain Covid's Origins," *New York Times*, January 25, 2025,

https://www.nytimes.com/2025/01/25/us/politics/cia-covid-lab-leak.html.

9 MELVILLE B. NIMMER, NIMMER ON FREEDOM OF SPEECH § 1.02(B), 1–12 (1984).

10 Alan M. Dershowitz, "Shouting 'Fire!'," *The Atlantic Monthly*, 263, no. 1 (Jan. 1989): 72.

11 For examples, see David Shih, "Hate Speech And The Misnomer Of 'The Marketplace Of Ideas'," *NPR*, May 3, 2017, https://www.npr.org/sections/codeswitch/2017/05/03/483264173/hate-speech-and-the-misnomer-of-the-marketplace-of-ideas, and Stanley Ingber, "The Marketplace of Ideas: A Legitimizing Myth," 1984 *Duke Law Journal* 1–91 (1984), https://scholarship.law.duke.edu/dlj/vol33/iss1/1.

12 Jacob Shamsian, "15 bewildering conspiracy theories that celebrities think are true," *Business Insider*, November 15, 2019, https://www.businessinsider.com/conspiracy-theories-celebrities-believe-2017–11 (listing Kyrie Irving, B.o.B., and Tila Tequila as flat earth adherents).

Argument #8: Free Speech Protects Power

1 A.J. Liebling, "The Wayward Press: Do You Belong in Journalism?," *New Yorker*, May 14, 1960, at 105, https://www.newyorker.com/magazine/1960/05/14/do-you-belong-in-journalism.

Argument #9: Misinformation and Disinformation Aren't Free Speech

1 *Gertz v. Robert Welch, Inc.*, 418 U.S. 323, 339–40 (1974).

2 376 US 254 (1964).

3 Samantha Barbas, "The Enduring Significance of *New York Times Co. v. Sullivan*," Knight First Amendment Institute at Columbia University, March 18, 2024, https://knightcolumbia.org/blog/the-enduring-significance-of-new-york-times-v-sullivan.

4 "Rudy Giuliani slams New York City major Bill de Blasio, black lives matter organization," *Fox News*, July 10, 2020, https://www.foxnews.com/transcript/rudy-giuliani-slams-new-york-city-mayor-bill-de-blasio-black-lives-matter-organization (Giuliani called BLM "a terrorist organization," "a violent organization," and "a racist organization" that is "actually participating in hate speech").

5 Cheryl Corley, "Black Lives Matter Fights Disinformation To Keep The Movement Strong," *NPR*, May 25, 2021, https://www.npr.org/2021/05/25/999841030/black-lives-matter-fights-disinformation-to-keep-the-movement-strong.

6 "Censorious governments are abusing 'fake news' laws," *The Economist*, February 13, 2021, https://www.economist.com/international/2021/02/13/censorious-governments-are-abusing-fake-news-laws.

7 Jacob Sullum, "Comentary: New research shows CDC exaggerated the evidence for masks to fight COVID," *Chicago Sun-Times*, February 8, 2023, https://chicago.suntimes.com/columnists/2023/2/8/23591132/cdc-exaggerated-evidence-supporting-mask-mandates-column-jacob-sullum.

8 Tim Stelloh, "ACLU files lawsuit over Puerto Rico 'fake news' laws feared by journalists covering pandemic," *NBC News*, May 20, 2020, https://www.nbcnews.com/news/latino/aclu-files-lawsuit-over-puerto-rico-fake-news-laws-feared-n1211516.

9 *Rodríguez-Cotto v. Vazquez-Garced*, No. 20-cv-01235 (D.P.R. May 19, 2020) (complaint), https://www.courthousenews.com/wp-content/uploads/2020/05/rodriguez_cotto_complaint_5–19-20_filing_final_1.pdf at para. 36.

10 Tim Stelloh, "ACLU files lawsuit."

11 Ibid.

12 *Rodríguez-Cotto v. Pierluisi-Urrutia*, 668 F. Supp. 3d 77, 110 (2023).

13 Ibid. at 104.

14 Nico Grant and Tiffany Hsu, "Google Finds 'Inoculating' People Against Misinformation Helps Blunt Its Power," *New York Times*, August 24, 2022, https://www.nytimes.com/2022/08/24/technology/google-search-misinformation.html.; Jon Roozenbeek et al., "Psychological Inoculation Improves Resilience against Misinformation on Social Media," *Science Advances* 8, no. 34 (August 24, 2022): eabo6254, https://www.science.org/doi/10.1126/sciadv.abo6254.

15 As quoted in Grant and Hsu, "Google Finds 'Inoculating' People." Jon Roozenbeek, Sander van der Linden, and Thomas Nygren, "Prebunking Interventions Based on 'Inoculation' Theory Can Reduce Susceptibility to Misinformation Across Cultures," *Harvard Kennedy School Misinformation Review* (February 3, 2020), https://misinforeview.hks.harvard.edu/article/global-vaccination-badnews/.

16 Gerry Greenstone, "The History of Bloodletting," *British Columbia Medical Journal* 52, no. 1 (January/February 2010): 12–14, https://bcmj.org/premise/history-bloodletting.

17 National Center for Chronic Disease Prevention and Health Promotion Office on Smoking and Health. "The Health Consequences of Smoking—50 Years of Progress: A Report of the Surgeon General." *Centers for Disease Control and Prevention*, 2014, https://www.ncbi.nlm.nih.gov/books/NBK294310/

("Kool menthol cigarettes, characterized by the cooling effect of this additive, were offered to nose and throat specialists to hand out to their patients 'suffering from colds and kindred disorders.') This is disinformation, of course, but the disinformation must have led to some amount of misinformation.

18 Neel Burton, "When Homosexuality Stopped Being a Mental Disorder," *Psychology Today*, June 24, 2024, https://www.psychologytoday.com/us/blog/hide-and-seek/201509/when-homosexuality-stopped-being-a-mental-disorder.

19 Pamela Weintraub, "The Doctor Who Drank Infectious Broth, Gave Himself an Ulcer, and Solved a Medical Mystery," *Discover*, April 8, 2010, https://www.discovermagazine.com/health/the-doctor-who-drank-infectious-broth-gave-himself-an-ulcer-and-solved-a-medical-mystery.

20 Jonathan Rauch, *The Constitution of Knowledge* (Brookings Institution Press, 2021), *excerpted in Persuasion*, June 28, 2021, https://www.persuasion.community/p/jonathan-rauch-the-constitution-of.

21 Learned Hand, "The Spirit of Liberty," speech delivered at "I Am an American Day," Central Park, New York City, May 21, 1944, available at https://www.thefire.org/research-learn/spirit-liberty-speech-judge-learned-hand-1944.

Argument #10: About the Holocaust and the Rwandan Genocide

1 Aryeh Neier, *Defending My Enemy: American Nazis, the Skokie Case, and the Risks of Freedom* (International Debate Education Association, 2012), at 3; new edition forthcoming from The New Press, September 2025: https://thenewpress.com/books/defending-my-enemy.

2 A. Alan Borovoy, *When Freedoms Collide: The Case for Our Civil Liberties* (Lester & Orpen Dennys, 1988 second edition), 50.

3 "Cophenhagen, Speech, and Violence," *New Yorker*, February 14, 2015, https://www.newyorker.com/news/news-desk/copenhagen-speech-violence.

4 *Abrams v. United States*, 250 U.S. 616, 630 (1919) (Holmes, J., dissenting).

5 Wiener, A. 1919. "Die Pogromhetze." *Im deutschen Reich* 25 (July/August), pp. 289–299 at 299, as cited in Cyril Levitt, "Under the Shadow of Weimar: What Are the Lessons for Modern Democracies?," in *Under the Shadow of Weimar: Democracy, Law, and Racial Incitement in Six Countries*, Louis Greenspan & Cyril Levitt, eds. (Praeger 1993), 33.

6 Neier, *Defending My Enemy*, at 167.

7 United Nations International Criminal Tribunal for Rwanda. "Three Media Leaders Convicted for Genocide." Press release, December 3, 2003. https://unictr.irmct.org/en/news/three-media-leaders-convicted-genocide.

8 *Prosecutor v. Nahimana*, Case No. ICTR-99–52-T, Judgment at 319 ¶ 955 (Int'l Crim. Trib. for Rwanda Dec. 3, 2003), https://ucr.irmct.org/LegalRef/CMSDocStore/Public/English/Judgement/NotIndexable/ICTR-99–52/MSC26797R0000541998.PDF. ("Hassan Ngeze on the morning of 7 April 1994 ordered the *Interahamwe* in Gisenyi to kill Tutsi civilians.")

9 *Prosecutor v. Nahimana*, Case No. ICTR-99–52-A, Appeals Judgment (hereinafter *Nahimana II*) (Int'l Crim. Trib. for Rwanda Nov. 28, 2007), https://ucr.irmct.org/LegalRef/CMSDocStore/Public/English/Judgement/NotIndexable/ICTR-99–52/MSC31299R0000555179.PDF.

10 E.g. Susan Benesch, *Vile Crime or Inalienable Right: Defining Incitement to Genocide*, 48 Va. J. Int'l L. 485 (2008), https://www.researchgate.net/publication/228149554_Vile_Crime_or_Inalienable_Right_Defining_Incitement_to_Genocide.

11 *Nahimana* (appeal), ICTR-99–52-A, p. 380 ¶ 18 (partly dissenting opinion of Judge Meron).

12 Amicus Curiae Brief of the Open Society Justice Initiative et al., *Prosecutor v. Nahimana*, Case No. ICTR-99–52-A (Int'l Crim. Trib. for Rwanda Dec. 15, 2006), https://www.justiceinitiative.org/uploads/0777227e-8c7c-4684–84ac-34175f508095/ictr-nahimana-amicus-brief-20061215.pdf.

13 *Nahimana II*, ICTR-99–52-A, p. 377 ¶ 10 (partly dissenting opinion of Judge Meron).

14 Law No 18/2008 of 23/07/2008 relating to the Punishment of the Crime of Genocide Ideology, promulgated October 2008; available at https://www.refworld.org/legal/legislation/natlegbod/2008/en/68627.

15 Andrea Scheffler, *The Inherent Danger of Hate Speech Legislation: A Case Study from Rwanda and Kenya on the Failure of a Preventative Measure* (Friedrich-Ebert-Stiftung, 2015), 68, https://library.fes.de/pdf-files/bueros/africa-media/12462.pdf.

16 Amnesty International, *Safer to Stay Silent: The Chilling Effect of Rwanda's Laws on "Genocide Ideology" and "Sectarianism"* (London: Amnesty International, 2010), 11, https://www.amnestyusa.org/wp-content/uploads/2017/04/afr470052010en.pdf.

17 *Safer to Stay Salent* at Chapter 4 (denunciations) and pp. 12 and 20 (false accusations).

18 *Safer to Stay Silent* at 20.

19 Scheffler at 73.

20 Charles Mironko, "The Effect of RTLM's Rhetoric of Ethnic Hatred in Rural Rwanda" in *The Media and the Rwanda Genocide*, edited by Allan Thompson, 125–135 (Pluto Press, 2007), 129 ("The first response to my questions was often a claim of ignorance of RTLM. Some professed to know nothing of its message or its role in inciting violence. Many informants told me that they did not listen to RTLM at all, either because they did not own radios (or had no batteries) or because they did not perceive themselves to be part of the target audience for this radio station.").

21 Scott Straus, "What Is the Relationship between Hate Radio and Violence? Rethinking Rwanda's 'Radio Machete,'" *Politics & Society* 35, no. 4 (2007): 609–637.

22 Ibid. at 611.

23 Richard Carver, "Broadcasting & Political Transition" in *African Broadcast Cultures: Radio in Transition*, edited by Richard Fardon and Graham Furniss (James Currey Ltd, 2000), 189.

24 Straus at 615.

25 "First Amendment Watch Roundtable: Richard Delgado Responds to Louis Michael Seidman," *First Amendment Watch*, June 27, 2018, https://firstamendmentwatch.org/first-amendment-watch-roundtable-richard-delgado-responds-to-louis-michael-seidman/ ("Of course free speech can be progressive, promote racial equality, human flourishing, and communities that understand and respect each other. But it can also be regressive, as with hate speech, bullying, and spreading malicious rumors on social media. In Rwanda it contributed to genocide. In Charlottesville, it enabled Nazis and white supremacists to parade in a peaceful college town, terrifying the residents and sowing confusion and even death.")

26 Ambrose Doskow and Sidney B. Jacoby, "Anti-Semitism and the Law in Pre-Nazi Germany," 3 *Contemporary Jewish Record* 498, September 1940, *available at* https://www.bjpa.org/content/upload/bjpa/4_an/4_Anti-Semitism_September-October_1940.pdf.

27 Eric Heinze, *Hate Speech and Democratic Citizenship* (Oxford University Press, 2016), 131–32.

28 *Gesetz zum Schutze der Republik* [Law for the Protection of the Republic], 1922, §4, http://www.documentarchiv.de/wr/repschutz_ges01.html.

29 See generally Oron James Hale, *The Captive Press in the Third Reich* (Princeton University Press, 1964).

30 Sara Twogood "The *Munich Post*: Its undiscovered effects on Hitler," *UCSB Oral History Project*, visited March 20, 2025, https://holocaust.projects.history.ucsb.edu/Research/Proseminar/saratwogood.htm.

Also see Ian Kershaw, *Hitler: 1889–1936 Hubris* (W.W. Norton & Company, 2000), 269–94.

31 Calvin University German Propaganda Archive, https://research.calvin.edu/german-propaganda-archive/posters1.htm, Item #6 (est. date 1927).

32 Ron Rosenbaum, "Hitler's Doomed Angel," *Vanity Fair*, September 3, 2013, https://www.vanityfair.com/news/1992/04/hitlers-doomed-angel.

33 Kershaw at 169; US Holocaust Memorial Museum, "Beer Hall Putsch (Munich Putsch)," *Holocaust Encyclopedia*, edited November 23, 2023, https://encyclopedia.ushmm.org/content/en/article/beer-hall-putsch-munich-putsch.

34 US Holocaust Memorial Museum, "Beer Hall Putsch (Munich Putsch)," *Holocaust Encyclopedia*, edited November 23, 2023, https://encyclopedia.ushmm.org/content/en/article/beer-hall-putsch-munich-putsch.

35 Frank Jordans, "Records show Hitler enjoyed special treatment in prison," *Seattle Times*, December 22, 2015, https://www.seattletimes.com/nation-world/records-show-hitler-enjoyed-special-treatment-in-prison/.

36 *New York Times Co. v. Sullivan*, 376 U.S. 254 (1964).

37 *Texas v. Johnson*, 491 U.S. 397 (1989).

38 *Miller v. California*, 413 U.S. 15 (1973).

39 *Counterman v. Colorado*, 600 U.S. 66 (2023).

40 *Id. See also* "FIRE statement on the Supreme Court decision in Counterman v. Colorado," *FIRE*, June 27, 2023, https://www.thefire.org/news/fire-statement-supreme-court-decision-counterman-v-colorado.

41 *Brandenburg v. Ohio*, 395 U.S. 444 (1969).

42 *See generally Nahimana II*, No. ICTR-99–52-A.

43 See generally Anne Sophie Heumesser and Peter von Eyben, *The Media and the Rwanda Genocide: An Assessment* (Copenhagen: International Media Support, 2003), https://www.mediasupport.org/wp-content/uploads/2012/11/ims-assessment-rwanda-genocide-2003.pdf, at 14 ("The cabinet took the final decision. The only radio-station, which got a license, was the soon famous RTLM.") and 16 ("RTLM regularly denounced opposition members and persons who were known to be critical towards the government as traitors, RPF-accomplices and enemies,").